The Garden of Your Mind

The Garden of Your Mind

REMOVING THE WEEDS OF
THIS WORLD FROM THE
GARDEN OF YOUR MIND

Dr. Reynald Joseph Williams

Enoch Publishing and Enterprises

Copyright © 2015 Dr. Reynald Joseph Williams
All rights reserved.

Unless otherwise stated, all Scripture quotations are taken from the King James Version New Scofield Study Bible.

ENOCH PUBLISHING AND ENTERPRISES
15500 Minerva Avenue
Dolton, Illinois 60419

ISBN: 0692567364
ISBN 13: 9780692567364

This book may not be reproduced in any form, stored in a retrieval system, or transmitted in any form by any means – electronic, mechanical, photocopy, recording, or otherwise –without prior written permission of the publisher, except as provided by United States of America copyright law.

Printed in the United States of America

Acknowledgments

I WISH TO EXPRESS MY deepest appreciation to my wife, Carolyn, for her constant support and encouragement.

To my dear children, Carlos, Teresa, Ayondela, Christopher, Curtis, Davis, Reynald II, Cecoria, Lynnece, Leah and Yahshua for the lessons I learned through them on being a spiritual father and for their not judging my shortcomings.

To my brother Kenneth for his continued encouragement and counsel when I wanted to quit.

To all of the saints who operate in the fivefold ministries that imparted spiritual wisdom into my life.

Contents

	Acknowledgments	v
	Introduction	ix
Chapter 1	Here's Mud in Your I—Self	1
Chapter 2	Here's Mud in Your Other I—Fear	10
Chapter 3	Kingdom Preschool	19
Chapter 4	The Facts of Life	29
Chapter 5	Dirt in Your I	38
Chapter 6	Wayward Instructions	47
Chapter 7	A Change of Heart	55
Chapter 8	Your Wilderness Test	63
Chapter 9	Draw Me, Lord	74
Chapter 10	A Need to Read	84
Chapter 11	Is He All the Way in Your Heart?	94
Chapter 12	You Are Not Alone	103
Chapter 13	Don't Play the Fool	111
Chapter 14	Just A.S.K.	119
Chapter 15	Spiritual Warfare—Your Armor	127
Chapter 16	Spiritual Warfare—Your Destiny	135
	Notes	145

Introduction

THERE ARE NUMEROUS RELIGIOUS WEEDS floating around in the wind of this world that enter the minds of believers. These weeds are hindering many from fully surrendering their lives to God. These weeds are blowing from their jobs, their families, their friends, and those whom they trust. The ecosystems of their environment have placed them on the threshold of death and destruction. No child of God is exempt from the potential effects this system could have on his or her life. There are saints who are straddling the fence of life; they are lukewarm and are lost in their churches. They are lost because the weeds of Satan have entered their minds. They don't believe that they have to study the Bible daily or attend weekly assemblies of the saints. However, they have no problem with watching their favorite television shows and sporting events for hours. They religiously read the written materials of this world's media. They have no problem with attending their jobs for a paycheck or attending social events with their friends.

The church has allowed the system of humans to dictate God's agenda—not for all of us, but enough to present a weaker witness to the world at large. According to the 2011 *Yearbook of American and Canadian Churches*[1], the Roman Catholic Church (No. 1) and The Southern Baptist Convention (No. 2) are still significantly larger than all other North American denominations, but Catholics posted minimal growth of less than 1 percent, and the southern Baptist membership fell for a third straight year.

The Ten Largest Christian Bodies

1. The Catholic Church: 68.5 million, up 0.57 percent
2. Southern Baptist Convention: 16.1 million, down 42 percent
3. The United Methodist Church: 7.8 million, down 1 percent
4. The Church of Jesus Christ of Latter-Day Saints (Mormon): 6 million, up 1.42 percent
5. National Baptist Convention (USA): 5 million, no membership updates reported
6. Evangelical Lutheran Church in America: 4.5 million, down 1.96 percent
7. National Baptist Convention of America: 3.5 million, no membership updates reported
8. Assemblies of God: 2.9 million, up 52 percent
9. Presbyterian Church (USA): 2.7 million, down 2.61 percent
10. The Church of God in Christ: 5.5 million, no membership updates reported

Source: February 14, *2011, Yearbook of American & Canadian Churches*

This means people are not being brought to the knowledge of the saving power of Jesus Christ. There could be, however, those who believe and are not in a church, but God's word states that we should forsake not the assembling of ourselves together (Heb. 10:24–25). We should be, every day, lifting up someone in his or her faith now more than ever before because of the signs of the time.

My ministry to numerous present and ex-church members has revealed that many of them left their previous churches because they had a disagreement with one person in their original church home or their feelings were bruised. Other disgruntled church goers took up residence at another church for the same reason and became non-active members. Not only that, but the systems of this world—the distance that many have to travel to and from their jobs and the time they are now required to spend on the job—have created a new generational type of Christian; they are positional and title driven. They are also the ones leaving their churches with the excuse that "Church leadership is out of touch with the ways of the world today and my needs." Or they say, "Why go to church? Church folk act just like those folk in the world." These individuals have focused their attention on people and not on Christ.

Psalms 92:12-13 reads: "The righteous shall flourish like the palm tree; he shall grow like a cedar in Lebanon. Those who are planted in the house of the Lord shall flourish in the courts of our God." So each of us must answer the question: "Have I been planted here to fulfill the purpose God has for me here, or am I a tumbleweed?"

If roots are not established, people "tumble in" when they want, and then "tumble out" when they want—usually taking others with them.[2] If you are not planted in a church, then you are a spiritual tumbleweed. Tumbleweed has a tendency to get caught on something, dry up, and eventually die. No moisture (ointment) is ever applied.

Some churches feed their members a smorgasbord of spiritual junk food while catering to the wants of the people and not to their spiritual needs and their spiritual maturity. Their members are getting fat on spiritual milk and are regurgitating the meat of the gospel. Their spiritual minds and souls are lacking the nourishment needed for this end-time battle with Satan. There are still others who do not believe Satan exists and have limited their view of him to a fictitious character that is red, has horns, and walks around with a pitchfork. This is also fed to us through the media. Each born-again believer, believe it or not, is on assignment for God and His kingdom. We have been called to go into the world and make disciples. We are to come out of our church building, become the church walking, and work in the vineyard of God – this earth - redeeming souls to His Kingdom. This means we must stop purchasing the things of this world. We must pursue His redeeming mercy every day and die to this world. Get ready to get planted by the Holy Spirit.

> And except those days should be shortened, there should no flesh be saved; but for the elect's sake those days shall be shortened.

Then if any man shall say unto you Lo, here is Christ, or there; believe it not. For there shall arise false Christs, and false prophets, and shall show great signs and wonders insomuch that, if it were possible, they shall deceive the very elect (*Matt. 24:22–24*).

This book has been written to spiritually remove the weeds of this world (Satan's kingdom) from the soil of your mind. Then you will be set free by the power of the Holy Spirit and move into a life-changing relationship with God. Learn about the religious weeds in life that hinder us from fully surrendering our life to God. Too many saints are lukewarm—on the fence, in the world, and lost in church. If you are not planted in a church, then you are a tumbleweed. Just as you tumbled into the church, you'll tumble out and roll to another. It is time to stop tumbling and stand so that the word of God can take root in your spirit. I strongly suggest that you keep your Bible near as you will be asked to read specific scriptures before moving forward with the reading of pursuing paragraphs and preceding thoughts.

CHAPTER 1
Here's Mud in Your I–Self

※

GARDENING IS NOTHING LIKE IT was years ago. Before the introduction of high-rise buildings and the industrial revolution, families lived close to the soil and close to one another. Herding, farming, and gardening were the great hallmarks of the *family* lifestyle. Children knew their responsibility was to rise early in the morning, feed the livestock, go to school, do their homework and work in the fields with their parents to plant, cultivate, and harvest their crop(s). Today the name *family* has taken on an oblique line, causing it to slant and slope. Our judicial system has removed the biblical meaning of family and has replaced it with its own. Nationally, marriage is legal between a man and another man. The community of human life—grandparents, uncles and aunts, nieces and nephews, friends, and even your enemies—are the products needed to assist with your physical, mental, and spiritual development. People's system of thought today has totally removed God from this equation. The seed of thought that we allow to take root in our subconscious—unannounced to us—will either draw us closer to God (the light) or will set up a carnal partition that blinds us from the truth (the light of God). When we allow this to happen, then we are found walking in darkness.

Now more than ever before, we must slow down and pay attention to our "mind talk," those thoughts that are spoken internally and unconsciously in the mind. Thoughts that cause people to unconsciously speak to themselves and act out on negative thoughts that condemn their souls. Thoughts that we tend to not pay attention to. Those thoughts that shape and form our destiny. "For as he thinketh in his heart, so is he: Eat and drink, saith he to thee; but his heart is not with thee" (Prov. 23:7). What are you rich in? Are you rich in love, joy, peace, long-suffering, gentleness, goodness, faith, meekness, and temperance? Or are you rich in adultery, fornication, hatred, strife, envying, murder, reveling, and drunkenness? You can determine this by focusing in on your thoughts. What thoughts occupy the majority of your thinking? When you start to pay attention to your thoughts, you will find out what kind of person you are. What we think we are is what we speak to the world in our actions and in our speech. Because we are so busy looking outside ourselves, we miss those spots, those wrinkles, and those blemishes that creep into our lives that darken our vision. Compare it to the first sighting of rust on a car. If the rust is not repaired immediately, you tend to ignore it and pay it no attention; and before long, you have a hole. Not only do you have a hole, but the rust color doesn't match the color of the paint on your car. If you say that you are a Christian, your life action and speech should reflect that to the world. As with all procrastination, just as we can ignore the rust on a car, we tend to also ignore the rusted condition of our spirit man. Today is your day to let God re-member and re-store you to His body.

So, how does this condition get fixed? Each of us needs to look at ourselves and see ourselves for what we really are—*dirt*. Yes, I said it, dirt. Lifeless dirt that has a soul and spirit (the life-giving attribute of God) rooted inside it—you. Without that life we return to dust—dirt. All dirt requires nutrients provided by the sun and nutrients provided by water. Our inner person, our soul, needs spiritual nutrients provided by the Father, His Son, and the Holy Spirit in order to mature. Gardeners and farmers seek out the best soil to plant productive seeds. It is rare to hear of a gardener or farmer deliberately planting weeds. Weeds are destructive to a garden. Their roots take over the soil and choke the roots of those plants that the gardener has planted. The words of Satan are like weeds. If you let them, they will choke off the good news of Christ and spread chaos in your mind.

Before we go on, I would like for you to read Matthew 13:3-9 and 11-23 out loud yourself before reading the next paragraph. Also, as we move forward, so that we will not have any confusion, the noun *man* used in these writings is applicable to both male and female.

"So God created man in his own image, in the image of God created He him; male and female created He them" (*Gen. 1:27*).

Just as there are specific soils that are best for growing organic product, there are spiritual soils that are best for growing spiritual fruit. If necessary, however, farmers will attempt to grow whatever crop they can in any soil that is available to them. When push comes to shove, *the crop (harvest) is the most important substance that the gardener and farmer are looking for.* As we progress through the pages of this book, I suggest that you put your flesh to the side and concentrate on your *soul*—the seed that God planted in you. Your outward image, your flesh, represents the decaying part of your person—this cursed earth. It is like the hull of a planted seed. That hull—your flesh—needs to die so that the spirit of God that is in *you* can germinate in the word of God and bring forth fruit. Your flesh is not eternal, but oh how much it loves itself, pampers itself, and esteems itself. Because of this, it becomes quite difficult for us to walk past a mirror. We want to look at ourselves (our flesh); we take selfies of our flesh to confirm to ourselves that we are presentable to the *world*. We want to be liked by the world. We want God to give us the desires of our hearts without a true commitment to serve Him. We don't want to make Him Lord of our life. We are happy with just being saved. Speaking of worlds, I have a segment devoted to this subject. Read on!

Today would be a good day for you to examine yourself (your inner thinking) and see what soil you are. Are you wayside soil, are you stony soil, are you thorny soil, or are you good ground soil? Let's be honest; you can't answer that question. The reason for this is because you haven't spent time with yourself. You have become intimately comfortable with who *you* think you are. To prove my point, right now, answer the following questions:

- What person do you fashion yourself and lifestyle after?
- What person do you attempt to emulate?
- What person do you admire the most?

If you did not answer Jesus Christ for all three of these questions, then you failed the test. The only way to past this test is to become intimately emerged in God's word. If all of us would be honest with ourselves, we don't live here solely to please God. We want something for ourselves, and that something is to be recognized and praised for our *perceived* accomplishments.

In looking at how media have highlighted people's outward appearance and works, and not the inner person (*the seed*), it becomes easy to see how an individual can be groomed to want to look good in physical appearance, in actions, and in deeds. One doesn't consider that when people make these their priority—(*pride*)—they are off-balance *mentally* and are walking on a tightrope that requires them to keep up this false appearance. But in reality, the higher they go with pride, the greater the fall, and trust me, there is no safety net.

Genesis 2:7 tells us: "And the Lord God formed man of the dust of the ground and breathed into his nostrils the breath of life; and man became a living soul."

God planted a seed in each and every one of us. If God had not breathed on us, we would not have life. We either cultivated ourselves with the Word of God, or we cultivate ourselves with the word of Satan. In order to cultivate one's self in the word of Satan, one has to abandon God's word," the life-giving force that God freely gives us. Weeds of destruction take root in the garden of our mind, and with that rooting, we will have consequences. What have we (humans) succumbed to that now pollinates our thoughts? What have we succumbed to that now aerates our soul? The answer is death. I'm not talking about the planting of a body in the ground after all physical life has been quenched from it. I'm talking about the true and eternal death, which is simply separation from God. These are two essential questions for the person who would be called a son of God. The first question is: "Are you studying the Word of God daily and allowing Him to breathe life into all situations in your mind garden?" The second question is: "Are you rightly dividing the word of truth in your mind garden?" "Study to show thyself approved unto God, a workman that needeth not to be ashamed, rightly dividing the word of truth" (*2 Tim. 2:15*).

As you look at your *external world* today, it would behoove you to take note of its condition, for if you do not stand and watch over your soul, this world's present state can corrupt your *internal world*, the world you live in inside yourself. No one lives there but you. All visitors to this domain are invisible. Your thoughts are the sole proprietor. I recall having a brief conversation with one of my neighbors regarding the police's responsibilities in the community. As he thought and talked to me about the responsibilities of our police department, he became very emotional (inwardly upset) about what *he* felt the police should be doing in and for the community (outwardly). Would I be correct to state that in your recent past, you have talked, discussed, and even debated with people about a given subject, and as they expressed what they inwardly felt about the subject, you saw a metamorphosis occur on the outside of them and they went from mild and meek Bruce Banner and turned into the *Incredible Hulk*? I'm sure you have, and believe it or not, they have witnessed the same metamorphosis in you. When people allow themselves to get internally angry about things they have no control over on the outside, they are subject to take their internal feelings and act out their frustration in a negative and destructive way externally.

Now let's imagine being in a park or in an open field on a nice, sunny day. A cool breeze is blowing, birds are singing their praises to God, your thoughts are clear and pure, and you are relaxed. Imagine being at a lake, a beach, or in the mountains near flowing water. Nature is calm, and you find yourself in a peaceful state. Can you feel the peace? Have you experienced a moment when you looked upon the face of a child, and because of the peace you saw on that child's face, for that short tiny moment, you felt it too? *Peace!* Our present-day social environment doesn't authorize peace. This world says it wants peace, but there is a constant pursuit for the next opportunity to be recognized—particularly by those who are striving for the same thing. Everybody wants to be recognized by someone, they want their opinion heard, they want the steady mental drug fix of feeling good about themselves without God. This is not peace; this is chaos!

Let me share with you an experience that I had with God. Many years ago I was invited to a wedding. After the ceremony the festivities were moved to another facility that had a bar. Note that this event took place in Chicago, Illinois, long before laws were placed on the books prohibiting smoking in buildings. As I sat with God at this event, He drew my carnal eyes to a baby girl, who was about four months old. The child's mother was holding her over her right shoulder. The baby was wide-awake with big, beautiful eyes doing what all of us do: she was canvassing her surroundings. I'm sure we know that a four-month-old child is very limited with his or her ability to intelligently engage with this type of noisy stimuli: cursing, loud music, people yelling at one another as they each attempted to be heard. And yes, the room was filled with cigarette smoke. God showed me in the spirit that this was the condition that was attempting to infect His body, the church, the body of Christ. With a continued intake of this world's stimuli and without a *committed* intake of God's word (spiritual cultivation), there will be a negative effect on this child's spiritual development. One can begin looking at spiritual truth through skewed lenses and totally not see God. All of us must be cognizant of this one fact. All of the darkness in the kingdom of Satan is seeking our attention, and it is the loudest voice in the room, the garden of your mind, your thoughts. Satan is constantly sending up smoke screens to hide his true intent.

Isaiah 26: 1–4 tells us: "In that day shall this song be sung in the land of Judah: We have a strong city; salvation will God appoint for walls and bulwarks. Open ye the gates that the righteous nation that keepeth the truth may enter in. Thou will keep him in perfect peace whose mind is stayed on thee because he trusteth in thee. Trust ye in the Lord forever; for in the Lord [God] is everlasting strength."

Yes, it is true. We all need saving—not just today but every day of our life. We need a wall of protection surrounding us, and all of us need God. Not a small g-o-d, but the God of all creation. Whose eyes are open to see it? What makes the city strong? Having someone watching the city. Salvation is the walls of your city, and the gates are your eyes. So *Jehovah* is the strength in the city of your mind. Now, what day is Isaiah talking about? When we accept Christ as our Lord and Savior, we enter into our day of rest. We rejoice and sing because we have no need to fear. We have moved into the city of the salvation of our God, and the gates are strong and mighty. We no longer have to fight with the enemy (Satan) because we now realize that the battle has already been won in Christ Jesus. But we do have to come out of ourselves and spiritual fight for the souls of those who are clueless that there is a spiritual fight going on for their souls.

Isaiah 12:1–5 reads: "O Lord, I will praise thee; though thou was angry with me, thine anger is turned away, and thou comfortedst me. Behold, God is my salvation; I will trust, and not be afraid; for the Lord even JEHOVAH [the Lord] is my strength and my song; he also is become my salvation. Therefore with joy shall ye draw water out of the wells of salvation and in that day shall ye say, Praise the Lord, call upon his name, declare his doings among the people make mention that his name is exalted. Sing unto the Lord; for he hath done excellent things. This is known in all the earth."

In your garden, when was the last time you sang God's praises? When was the last time you drank from His well of salvation and were drunk from rejoicing in God's forgiveness of your sins? When was the last time you shared the good news (the gospel) of Jesus Christ, our Lord and Savior, with a friend, an enemy, your neighbor, or a coworker? If we are truthful with ourselves, our answer would be *"not enough, not lately."* And the reason we must answer in this way is because we have not submitted 100 percent to the spiritual pruning of the weeds of wickedness in our own mind's garden. Pride, self-centeredness, jealousies, uncleanness, and the like have taken root, and we have become more accustomed to hearing from a weed than hearing from God's word. When this occurs, we develop satanic strongholds.

Like Satan, we want more than is due us. Like Eve, we seek the physical and not the spiritual. Like Adam, we are ashamed of ourselves but take pride in worshiping our false god—*self*. So in our mind we hide; our eyes are closed from seeking God and from ministering to one another. We have become comfortable with the darkness sin brings into our mind, and the spiritual decay it brings to our spirit man. The present condition of the world is a direct reflection of the condition of people's souls, but we are not willing to look. People are not subduing. People have become subdued.

What day was it when *Isaiah 26:1–4* was sung in your Judah? Let me reword this for you. What day was it when *Isaiah 26:1–4* was sung in your praise? Can you imagine the impact your praise has in your garden? Many cannot. They cannot praise because they have been punctured with the cares of life—bills, marriage, children, jobs, and sickness, to name a few. They live on what they see in the natural, which is dying, and not on what is spiritual, which is eternal. They have accepted the natural things of life and have rejected the spiritual. Because of this, their eyes are tuned to darkness and can only witness to death, not life. It is my sincere belief that a revival is on the horizon. *Acts 2:17* tells us: "And it shall come to past in the last days, saith God, I will pour out of my Spirit upon all flesh; and your sons and your daughters shall prophesy, and your young men shall see visions, and your old men shall dream dreams." Can your see it happening right now?

So many in the church have flushed rap music down the proverbial toilet. Yes, it started out as a violent way for today's youth to express themselves, but the system of humans created that pathway. In the church I have come across numerous gospel rap artists who rap only for God. Some have been raised in the church, while others have just recently found Christ and have accepted Him as their Lord and Savior. Sound like anyone you know? They are seeking God for their very life. In other words, they are seeking God more than many of us old church heads. This is because so many of us have not stayed abreast of the deeper revelations of God that are being poured out on the earth today. We are locked in to tradition, like the Pharisees and the Sadducees were in the days that Christ walked this earth—that is, how we dress, what we can and cannot eat, where we can go, and whom we can and cannot talk to. God has moved on, and we are not willing to change, to go deeper in God's word, and to mature. Just think about it for a minute. Gospel music today is a mixture of jazz, R&B, funk and rock, and we have no problem with it. Like Rap, it came out of a need for us to express ourselves at that time.

God is preparing to prune this world, for the harvesting of souls is at hand. The sickle is now ready to cut deep into the garden of your mind for a harvest that is eternally pleasing to God. Each of us must now give up all of those historical church traditions that were added to please someone else's need for power. Like the Pharisees and Sadducees in the Old Testament who knew the law but not its intent, we must *now* be willing to submit all of the selfish-individual-nature, the *sin* in our mind garden to God and be saved. (*Salvation is a day-by-day process.*) The winds of wickedness blow 24/7, and with that wind, the weeds of spiritual decay are attaching themselves to every soul that they can. Eve blamed the serpent, and Adam blamed God. Who are you blaming for your spiritually deprived condition? Is it your father, your mother, another relative, a friend, your teacher, the government, your past experiences? Who are you hiding behind? Who are you using to justify why you act like you act, why you drink like you drink, why do you curse, why do you fornicate, and why do you sin? Everyone wants to be politically correct in today's society. Few want to be *biblically correct*.

As you study the following chapters in this book, I declare that you will be set free of the weeds that have been planted in the garden of your mind. It is my sincere prayer that as you absorb the pages of this book and catch a hunger to read God's word daily, you will allow the Spirit of God to blow a newness and a refreshing hard breeze into you to rekindle the spiritual flame in you as when you first believed. He wants to remove all of this world's mud from your I if you let Him. He will peel the mud from your soul so that your spirit man can see clearly. So the question for all of us is: "Who is in control, you or the Spirit of God?" When you surrender to the Holy Spirit, He will remove all of the mud in your I—self.

CHAPTER 2
Here's Mud in Your Other I—Fear

§

And Ahab told Jezebel all that Elijah had done, and how he had slain all the prophets with the sword.

Then Jezebel sent a messenger unto Elijah, saying, so let the gods do to me, and more also, if I make not thy life as the life of one of them by tomorrow about this time.

And when he saw that, he arose, and went for his life, and came to Beer-sheba, which belongeth to Judah, and left his servant there.

But he himself went a day's journey into the wilderness, and came and sat down under a juniper tree. And he requested for himself that he might die, and said, "It is enough! Now, O Lord, take away my life; for I am not better than my fathers" (*1 Kings 19:1–4*)

THIS SCRIPTURE IS A GREAT illustration of what can happen when we allow our inward voices to manipulate our outward action. In chapters 17 and 18 of 1 Kings, Elijah stopped the rain, God fed Elijah, and God had Elijah bring life back into a widow's son. God showed Himself mighty and consumed the offering of the evening sacrifice with fire. After all that Elijah saw God do through him, Elijah still found himself listening to those inward voices in his mind. He allowed an outside event—Jezebel's threat to kill him—to bring fear into his inward parts.

So often, like Elijah in this event, we allow what we hear, what we think, what we think people are saying about us, what we see, and what negative things we say about ourselves to paralyze our ability to function. We need to find the root to this thinking and uproot it.

As children, we have heard our friends, family members, and others say not too amiable things about us that impacted our character in a negative way. Now as adults, those negative characteristics are wedged in our subconscious, and periodically they rise and attempt to take dominion in our thinking. They solicit a response from our emotion, and before we know it, we are running from ourselves. We are quick to forget that there is a battle for our mind waged against us by Satan. If we refuse to go on the offense in this battle, we will fall prey to Satan's attacks, and he will drain our strength to fight right out of us. If we stay like this for too long, we could faint. If we stay in this condition too long, we could wither up and die. Never turn your back to your enemy. He will hit you in your head.

Consider a pastor who has preached a sermon that brought deliverance to many in the congregation; that pastor cannot let his guard down in his study because temptation stands just outside the door. Like Christ, after this pastor has had virtue (energy) drained from him, he is now weak. Satan always comes after the battle to collect the weak, the sick, and the wounded. We have to always operate like Christ, immediately retreat to our prayer closet—our *war room*—and get reenergized by the Holy Spirit. It is this regeneration that strengthens us for Satan's next attack. It is this regeneration that puts the patchwork to our spiritual armor so that we can stand against another Satanic bombardment in our inner thinking.

Now catch this. Elijah operated like a general for the Lord when he won the battle against the prophets of Baal. Elijah strutted himself before the people, and God used Elijah to reveal Himself to the people. After the revelation of God was revealed to His people and to the prophets of Baal, Elijah had the prophets of Baal put to death. God expects us to remove all wickedness from the garden of our mind – from our eye sight. We know that there is a God, but few are willing to follow Him. So many today pursue the lifeless visible gods of this world who, like the gods of Jezebel, have no power.

When the messenger of Jezebel informed Elijah of her intentions, Elijah feared, and he ran for his life. We see two events here played out in one. Whenever we accomplish an assignment in the earth realm for God, there will be a reaction by Satan in the earth realm against us. With Elijah's victory, he became vulnerable. With Jezebel's defeat, she became dangerous.[1] Elijah's victory kindled the viciousness of Jezebel, and with the viciousness, Elijah felt he had to flee for his life. It is interesting how vulnerable we are when we are loved by everyone and how weak we become when we find out that those who loved us are now our foe.

Our sometime inability to stay consistent with our kingdom work for God causes many to ask, "Where is your faith?" "What are you afraid of?" Sometimes our *now* does not line up with the *now* of God. "Now faith is the substance of things hoped for, the evidence of things not seen" (Heb. 11:1). To be truly a force for God, one must have faith—not in the visible, but in the invisible. Let me give you an example. Years ago someone wanted a better way to get from one place to another. His want was realized when he invented the wheel.[2] It is thought that the first wheels were pottery wheels. But the invention of the wheel wasn't as important as the invention of the axle, which connects the wheel to a platform. Think about it for a moment. It is impossible to ride on a wheel. The axle and a platform had to be constructed first, giving the wheel the ability to support objects of different sizes and weights.

The idea was always there; we just needed someone to *create* all of its components. This is where our ability to subdue the earth is realized. When we align our will to the perfect will of God, we find ourselves drawing our needs to us. When our wheel is aligned with the will of God, we can move mountains. We can calm the raging sea. We then can overcome our other I — fear.

> And it came to pass, when Solomon had finished the building of the house of the Lord, and the king's house, and all Solomon's desire which he was pleased to do,

That the Lord appeared to Solomon the second time, as he had appeared unto him at Gibeon.

And the Lord said unto him, I have heard thy prayer and thy supplication that thou has made before me; I have hallowed this house, which thou hast built, to put my name there forever; and mine eyes and mine heart shall be there perpetually.

And if thou wilt walk before me, as David, thy father, walked, in integrity of heart, and in uprightness, to do according to all that I have commanded thee, and wilt keep my statutes and mine judgments [ordinances],

Then I will establish the throne of thy kingdom upon Israel forever, as I promised to David, thy father, saying, there shall not fail thee a man upon the throne of Israel (*1 Kings 9:1–5*).

"What do you really need?" The only answer that I can apply to the question is God's will for your life. It is God that enables each of us to achieve, accomplish, and do all that He wants to have us do in the earth realm. As He draws us to Him, we make ourselves ready to receive the gifts and talents that He wants to give us to use for the building of His kingdom. This is our purpose. If we have not prepared, if we are not ready to take responsibility for these gifts, God will not give them.

That chair that you sit on, the house or apartment that you live in, the airplane that people fly in, and the bed that you sleep on weren't made; they were created. These things did not exist until someone brought them into existence through the thought processes of their mind. The idea for these objects was conceived in someone's mind. Through trial and error, they brought something that was invisible into the earth realm—the natural. They took a creative thought—something not seen—and made it something seen. Solomon's ability to create the environment that he lived in by committing to God opened the door for not only his elevation in the kingdom of God and on earth, but to a greater degree, the elevation of his offspring as well. His obedience to God opened the door for generational blessings. What are you creating?

Like Solomon, we cannot allow the negative inward voices to cause us to lose focus and stop creating the environment God wants to dwell in. God has given all of us the ability to see into the spiritual realm. Too many, however, don't know how to look, and if they know how, they choose not to look. Our wants tend to outweigh our needs. Each and every day of our lives, we need more and more of God in our life. We have to start today to build for God first; He is already building our future.

Please note that Solomon put God's house in order before he built his own house. God wants to dwell in you. You are His house. *Putting God's house in order gives you the blueprint for the building of your house*—your family. How is the building of God's house in you coming along? Have you stopped construction because you are using more of your finances on your carnal house? Have you abandoned His house because you can't see the profitability in completing the construction? Or have you almost finished it, but you have neglected to furnish it with kingdom treasures? Whatever your reason is, you have to go back and finish. Remember, you cannot give up now. Your eternity depends on your completing your earthly assignment. Don't be afraid. Satan knows of your fear, and he wants to give you a *stop-construction notice*. He will present to you all the *politically correct* laws that saturate this earth realm in an attempt to stop your momentum. He will present to you all of the human-made spiritual dos and don'ts to hinder your progress. In short, he wants to take your power by convincing you to give it to him.

Let me help some of you here. The only thing that Satan can offer you is *hell*. Many are feeling the torment of hell when they allow Satan to pour seeds of doubt, mistrust, fear, loneliness, insecurity, hatred, and death into their mind garden. Satan loves to take those images of your childhood that were demonic and devastating to your self-esteem and remind you constantly of your shortcomings, your flaws and failures. This is why you cannot rest in your self-potential. Satan loves it when you take every negative act against you personally. When you do that, you give him power over you.

It is not your job to go around attempting to change how someone thinks and feels about you. Your job is to love others and live a life pleasing for God. You cannot serve God and man. You cannot please God and man. When you serve God and when you please God, those individuals who are drawn to God will be drawn to you. You then will have a platform and the wheels to share your love for God, for Jesus Christ, and for the Holy Spirit with them. It is your sincerity and honesty that will cause their other I—their fear and their emotions—to become focused on the things of the kingdom of God and not on the things of the kingdoms of this world.

EMBRACE YOUR JUDAS

Judas Iscariot, son of Simon as stated in *John 12:4*, is a figure in the New Testament that represents much of the betrayal in the world in this century. As with Judas, a wolf in sheep's clothing, many today have willfully accepted and are operating in his role in the church. His betrayal of Jesus sets him up as the villain and deserving of the way in which he met his end. Read *Psalms 41:9, John 13:18*, and *Acts 1:16*. As you can see, Judas had a role to play in the death, burial, and resurrection of Jesus. He just didn't know it. He may have seen Jesus as a way to fill his pocket, as we will see shortly.[3] Others say that he was part of a terrorist group called Sicarius, which in Latin means "murder." Sounds like Isis to me. If you don't mind, let me take a few minutes to paint a clearer picture of this man.

In *John 6:70*, Jesus answered them, "Have not I chosen you twelve, and one of you is a devil?" Please note that Jesus handpicked Judas to be one of his twelve disciples (an adversary). Whenever we conceive alternative motives against the plans of God, we operate in the realm of Satan and not in the realm of God, as with Judas. Jesus's sole purpose was to fulfill the purpose of God. As Jesus's purpose is to redeem man back to God, Judas also had a purpose. He didn't know it at the time, but his purpose was to be the betrayer. God knows the plan for your life. Do you? You can if you seek God first. Judas's focus on the things of this earth made him a betrayer. When we lose focus on our purpose, we betray God. When we seek the pleasures of this world and do not live to please God, we betray Him. Each of us must determine how we want to profit.

> Then entered Satan into Judas, surnamed Iscariot, being of the number of the twelve. (*Luke 22:3*)

When we don't pay attention to our inner voice, the voice of God calling us into obedience, we are subject to make the same mistake as Judas. As Judas was predestined for his purpose, we all are predestined too. In regard to the voice that we listen to, we must really pay attention to what the voice requests from us. Judas was a thief, according to *John 12:6*. Satan is a thief, according to *John 10:10*. Both of them reasoned with themselves on what they would do. They reasoned within themselves to operate outside of the will of God but did not know that they were operating in God's will. Because of his disobedience, Judas hung himself (*Matt. 27:5*); his body fell from the tree, and his midsection busted open (*Acts 1:18–19*). Because of his disobedience, Satan fell from his position in the kingdom of God and now suffers eternal damnation. Like a tree he was cut down (*Isa. 14:12*).

Even though Judas repented of his action and gave the money back to the chief priest and elders, his inner man would not allow him to forgive himself. That is what a mind will do that yields to the will of Satan. Listening to your inner man and not to God can cause you to relive and feed on your past mistakes. Feeding on your mistakes, like Judas, will cause you to hang yourself—not necessarily in the physical, but in your emotions. You have to develop a game plan. Like in football, you have to come up with an audible. Like in business, you have to create a contingency plan. Why not? Satan has his. Remember, Satan has been at this kill, still, and destroy business far longer than you have been saved and born again. He knows your desires, and he knows your wants better than you do. He will always visit you with a proposition to satisfy your inner man. You have to know that outward satisfaction leads to internal destruction. Satan will give your flesh a proposal that it will not want to refuse. His ability to tempt you is off the chart. You have to learn how to give all of that to Jesus. Follow the example of Jesus and give yourself to God, not Satan.

Myopia

How you see things and your way of thinking about things will impact your destiny. To have myopia means to be nearsighted or shortsighted. When what people are looking at or thinking about falls short of their retina, be it physical or spiritual, it causes them to see things out of focus. You tend to not be able to see the bigger picture. I call it *broken focus*, and I will cover it in more detail in chapter 10. But the point for now is for us to see normally. Some have to use corrective lenses, or the condition only affects one I—what you are looking at (self), or what you are thinking (fear). In an effort to get the mud out of your thinking I, you have to die to yourself I.

Elijah, Solomon, and Judah all had spiritual myopia. They could not see the whole plan of God. We have spiritual myopia because we can't see the whole plan of God. God wants us saved. He wants us to be with Him in eternity, but we can't see the end of what His plan is. Each of us has areas in our lives that have been darkened by our past. Because of this painful darkened past, we sometimes refuse to have the Holy Spirit clean us up so that we can stand in our deliverance. Elijah had Jezebel, Solomon had his women, and Moses had his speech. These betrayers were in their lives to keep them off focused. What is in your I that has caused you to turn to the things of this earth and not to the things of God?

God continues to send us what we need to draw us closer to Him. All we have to do is stop, stand, and let the Holy Spirit work like an axle on our myopia condition. He will show us how to build a platform of faith that will withstand the weight of our trials and tribulations. He will clear our vision so we can see the horizon of our deliverance. Then, as God leads us, we can be moved by Him in the direction that He wants us to go. Take the time today to have the mud removed from your other I. Take the time today to have your spiritual retina checked by the Holy Spirit. He has the tools to construct in you the visual lenses that you need to see your purpose and your destiny. He is titled the Comforter because that is who He is. He will repair your spiritual retina and cover your vision with His glory. When the healing process is complete, He will remove the bandages of healing so that you can focus correctly. His light and His revelation power will give you a clear impression of who He is and who you are in Him. You will be able to see truth like never before. The dark veil of Satan will be surgically removed and the mud will be removed from your other I, and you will live.

CHAPTER 3
Kingdom Preschool

§

"Train up a child in the way he should go and when he is old he will not depart from it" (*Prov. 22:6*).

WHEN I JOINED THE UNITED States Air Force and went to basic training, which is exactly what I got: *basic training*, I had to start at the beginning and learn a new way of doing things. Even though my parents had taught me how to think for myself, clean my room, wash my clothes, cook, and clean the house, the military was about to take me deeper into the processes of doing those things. Like the child I talked about in chapter 1, I and the other airmen assigned to our squadron were mere infants in an environment we had never been in before. We were to be trained and given the basic skills on marching, following orders, and working as a team. We were even taught how to fold our underwear, how to make our beds to the degree that you could bounce a quarter off them, how to place our clothing in a closet so that the closet was uniformed, and we learned how to truly clean a large floor to the point that you could eat on it. Much of our training was presented to us through training manuals, training tapes/movies, slide presentations, and direct frontal contact with the highly testosterone training instructors. We got up early and went to bed late. We ate together, ran together, exercised together, studied together, and yes, even took showers together. Our training instructor's sole purpose was to break each of us down to our lowest denominator and build us up into a highly functional member of a team. We could not show any signs of weakness, or the training instructor became our personal friend, if you know what I mean. He or she did everything legal to break us down. As a flight leader, I was set back two weeks in basic training for standing next to a supply shed and singing.

If you doubted yourself in any area of your military development, it was the training instructor's job to push you until you broke. If you didn't break, you graduated. If you broke, you were out. If you followed to the letter all of the requirements demanded of you, you were sure to pass and move on to your new assignment for more training, instruction, development, and testing. This process continued throughout my time in the military.

So many of us have joined the army of the Lord but have failed basic training. Like many in the armed forces who missed their mommy or just never grew up, many Christians, without realizing it, miss their carnal past. They don't want to take instruction, and they don't want to learn anything new because it requires discipline. Too many of us have come to believe that we are mature enough now that we don't need the word of God anymore. Just look with Eve. She enthusiastically went after a false word. If we are not careful, like the seeds in *Matthew 13*, we tend to return to what is familiar to us and comforts us in the natural. It is all about what is natural. This is true with the drug addict, the incarcerated, and with many of the children of God.

Did you know that the first school of learning was designated to be in the home? Most children are not comfortable leaving the safety of their home. Home should be where a foundation of individuality and oneness with God is set for the child. Home is where biblical understanding should be taught and practiced. "Preschoolers have a lot of fears. That's because they're often doing something they haven't done before."[1] When children do not know who they are, when they are shy, they will break from the true path and stifle their future potential. That's why some children cry when they are separated from their parents on their first day in preschool—a time to explore and learn a new environment. If they develop a lack of security within themselves, they are subject to resist the movement to mental and emotional maturity. I use the word maturity and not grown for a reason.

I believe that we never grow up, but we should be continuously maturing. You see, when you felt grown in your parent's house you felt that there were instructions from them that you no longer needed to follow. This meant that you felt that you were ready to operate in life independent from them even though you had no job, you had no money, you had no house – but you were grown in your own eyes. You felt that you have all the answers for your life. A mature person who is always maturing understands that they don't have all of the answers to life. So it should be with a Christian. We are not grown, God is taking us through steps to mature us into the vessels that He wants us to be. Adam and Eve failed to wait on their Heavenly Father to mature them.

Back to developing a lack of security within one's self. They are subjet to resisting the movement to mental and emotional maturity. This same process has occurred in the church and in the spirit for some of us. People are joining the church – the family of God - who are unfamiliar with the church culture; some become frightened and resist. They hear the gospel, but they can't internalize it so that they become God's Word – His voice. They speak kingdom words of God and the kingdom words of man. They continue to act like the world and not like God. They continue to speak like the world and not like God. It is as if world titles, positions, and talents are the foundations in their mind. This practice has caused many babes in Christ to be spiritually unbalanced. Being in that environment for an extended period of time can seal their fate. *How can someone who is spiritually ill in sin aid someone else who is also spiritually ill in sin?*

Like children, even though Adam and Eve had sinned against God's instructions, they had the God-given responsibility to train and develop their children—Abel, Cane, and Seth, to name a few—in the instructions laid down by God for mankind. But they were already sick with the illness of sin in their lives. They separated themselves from God, the source of their existence. *Please note that as God had formed man from the earth and created man in His image* (Gen. 1:26), in his own image man was given the ability to also create, produce seed from the earth within himself. Today as in the time of Adam, we are to instruct our children as God instructs us. We are not only to instruct them until they are able to follow the instructions of God on their own, but more importantly, our lives, coupled with the Word of God, are to be their manual for life. Somewhere along this process, man ignored this responsibility and moved uncontrollably to the creating part (sex) and disregarded the responsibility to mature their offspring in God's way of life. Man moved from spirit to flesh and has not looked back. Man is also allowing the world of men, who are manipulated by Satan, to train and develop his offspring.

When you look back on history, you see how as man became more interested in self (*self-pride*) and began to seek the so-called treasures of this world (*personal wealth*) and not the treasures of God (*holiness*), the training of the child took on a sinister matrix. As sin became the matrix for self-righteousness, self-righteousness became the matrix for more self-indulgence, and as more self-indulgence became the matrix for self-centeredness, self-centeredness became the matrix for pure evil. Have you ever noticed how evil can always be identified because it takes or makes an attempt to take what does not belong to it? Satan has always attempted to duplicate himself in the flesh of man, replace God's image with his own. Why is this? Because man was created in God's image and if Satan can rule man, he believes he can rule God. He believes that if he can decimate (destroy) a portion of God's creation, he will show his falsified power, and all of mankind will follow him. What do you think? The games of this life today are working overtime to desensitize our offspring to God so that what is not normal in the eyes of God becomes normal in their eyes. Without the morals of God to guide them, whatever they feel like doing at the moment, whatever they can do to satisfy the lust of their flesh, their pride for life, and the lust of the world, even if it isn't right, it becomes right to them.

Lot's Three-Step Program to Family Destruction

> "And Lot lifted up his eyes, and beheld all the plain of Jordan, that it was well watered everywhere before the Lord destroyed Sodom and Gomorrah, even as the garden of the Lord, like the land of Egypt as thou comest unto Zoar" (*Gen. 13:10*). The first step.

The name *Lot* in Hebrew means "covering or veil." We define this word in regard to protecting something: paint covering a wall or a rug covering a gouge in a floor; or to hide something: to cover up a mistake or to cover one's self in case something goes wrong. Lot covered himself in pride and self-glory when he chose the plain of Jordan. It wasn't God's glory on Lot. Lot covered himself in his own glory. It was all about himself. He saw a garden in the natural, but in the spiritual, he had just obtained a land full of spiritual weeds. When we look to self and move away from the covering of God, we become uncovered, and we begin to descend.

The word *Jordan* in Hebrew means "descend," "to go downward," "the enemy," "to fall." *Zoar* means "to be small," "be brought down." Because Lot was small in his thinking, he chose to go down into the enemy's camp with his spiritual eyes closed. Not only did *he* run toward destruction; he ran toward destruction in a small place where his enemies were, and he took his family with him. How often have you heard the idiom "The grass always looks greener on the other side of the fence"? Lot's life gives us a panoramic view of what sin does to you. If we are not careful, you will operate like a cow or a sheep, always reaching through the fence to get to the unreachable grass. You believe what someone else has is better than what you have, so you want it.

Lot is a testament to that fact. He didn't hear God tell him to lift up his eyes like God told Abram in *Genesis 13:14*. Lot lifted up his own eyes and made a decision without seeking God first. Whenever we lift up our eyes to the weeds of greed and the weed of pride, we walk in blindness and cannot see the true glory and purpose God has prepared for our life and the lives of our children. Remember, self-glory is self-centeredness; it is childish and produces only weeds. Yes, the plain of Jordon was well watered but only with natural water; the waters of the Spirit of God did not flow there. Yes, Lot was able to eat well and take care of his family in the natural, but he had no substance for his spirit man and the spiritual needs of his family. Lot felt no need to daily take of the spiritual food of God and feed it to his family. If it had not been for his uncle Abram (family), Lot and his daughters too would have been lost when Sodom and Gomorrah were destroyed by God. Lot chose to stay in the toddler state of his spiritual maturity.

Every teenager I know wants to be grown-up so they can do what they want to do. They don't want the restrictions that their parents put on them. They want independence—so they think. They don't realize that in moving away from one dependence, they move toward another. Let me put it to you like this: If you are not under the covering of God, whose covering are you under?

God doesn't want grown children. God wants spiritually mature children. There is a difference. When someone says to you, "I'm a grown man," or "I am a grown woman," he or she is really saying, "You can't tell me what to do." Spiritually mature people, with the guidance of the Holy Spirit, have elevated themselves and understand that they do not have all the answers to life; God does. They give their lives to God, and He leads them to green pastures. The grown-up person only sees himself or herself. Nothing comes before satisfying himself or herself. Not even God. Not realizing that they don't have all the answers, they limit themselves from maturing because, like the toddler, maturing will take them into the unknown—a fear that they must conquer for Christ.

Proverbs 30:7–9, which was written by Agur and Lemuel to God, says: "Two things have I required of thee; deny them not to me before I die: Remove far from me vanity and lies; give me neither poverty nor riches; feed me with food convenient for me, Lest I be full and deny thee and say,

Who is the Lord? Or lest I be poor and steal and take the name of my God in vain."

When we sit in the school of the pride of the eye, our vanity becomes our downfall. Lot, who wanted earthly riches, saw in his mind's eye the perceived opportunity to make a name for himself. Lot had flocks, herds, and tents. This meant that he had acquired some earthly wealth. He was so carnally removed from his true godly calling that he set out to make his own calling. Have you ever noticed how selfish toddlers can be? Everything belongs to them, and they will not share. If they are playing with one of their own toys and see another child playing with a different toy, the first child will get upset and want the second child's toy. The first child will even fight the second child for the toy, and if the first child gets the toy, he or she will soon lose interest in it and seek something else. Even after the child has lost interest in the second toy, he or she will guard it and attempt to keep other children from playing with it. *It takes wise parents—who are watchful— to come alongside the first child to train him or her in giving and not possessing.* Let the Holy Spirit come in to train and assist you in this area today.

Lot was not content with his wealth in his flocks, his herds, and his tents; he wanted all of what he thought was the good land, all that his carnal eyes could see. Lot's actions show us that not being able to give or share is a toddler move for an adult. To see this behavior in the body of Christ is not a proper testimony for the world to witness. Like Agur and Lemuel, all of us should be content with what we have. If not, the spirit of greed stands at the door of our mind garden and will plant seeds of covetousness. We will become addicted to material things, not to the spiritual things of God. Yes, God's plan for our lives is to give us riches, but we must seek the right riches. God wants us to purchase wisely, not foolishly. So, what riches are you gathering to yourself? Be honest! Are they earthly, or are they spiritual?

> "Abram dwelt in the land of Canaan and Lot dwelt in the cities of the plain, and pitched his tent toward Sodom" (*Gen. 13:12*). The second step.

When greed enters into your mind garden, you find yourself camping in the cities of abomination, not in the land flowing with milk and honey. You will place your tent (your body, your soul, and the body and soul of your family) at the door of wickedness and in the arms of darkness. Lot's mind garden never matured in the knowledge of the things of God. Lot lived horizontally, not vertically. Like Lot, many grown toddlers will look for and find temporary comfort in the things of this world. Unless they have correct and continuous training in the way of God, they will never mature. Unless God allows some dramatic event to arrest their attention, they will always reject the need for God in their lives. This is called a reprobate mind. God wants to build a hedge of protection around them, but they want to be fenced in by Satan. They will leave the safety of God's authority and protection to reach through the fence that Satan built in order to get to the decaying fruit of a dying world. They will even do patchwork on the fence when the word of God begins to punch holes in the lies Satan has caused them to believe. When someone presents the light of Christ, the good news of the Gospel to them, they retreat back into the darkness behind the fence because that is the purpose of the fence that Satan built. Their deliverance requires them to willingly have their flesh circumcised, crucified and exposed to the light of Christ. This deliverance can only come through prayer and fasting and will be painful to their flesh.

> "And they made their father drink wine that night: and the firstborn went in and lay with her father and he perceived not when she lay down when she arose" (*Gen. 19:33*). The third step.

All children have a tendency to backslide every now and then. Sin is like a cancer in the mind garden of a carnal Christian and in the mind garden of an unbeliever. Just as God has a family of sons and daughters, Satan too has a family of unbelievers. If you continue down to *Genesis 19:14*, you will see how low Lot's authority had fallen, not only in the city, but more importantly, with his family. When he came to his son-in-laws and instructed them to leave the city of Sodom for it was about to be destroyed, they felt that he was mocking them. Lot's failure to plant the laws and ordinances of God into his family's mind soil religiously caused him to lose them. Because Lot had not committed his life to God, the seldom godly example he presented before them did not germinate or generate a desire in them to know God for themselves. Because Lot's daughters were not raised in the culture and environment of God, they were more interested in the culture and environment in which they were raised.

If the child I talked about in my introduction is left to continue in the environment she was in, like Lot's daughters, she will have no problem doing what she saw adults do in her own carnal eyes. She will believe that her actions are right. Lot's daughters failed to seek and honor God but were willing followers in the ways of the world. Doesn't this sound like some individuals in the church—Christ's bride sometimes? She is yet prostituting herself before the world. She is losing her ability to birth children for the kingdom of God but is producing fatherless children for the kingdom of Satan. Like the children of Israel, each generation seems to grow weaker and not seek God. Many today don't even know who God is, nor do they care. They know of Him, but they don't know Him for themselves. Only a small remnant remains. God will always raise up a remnant, a standard that will not walk in the ways of the world. Are you that remnant?

Have you heard the idiom "An apple doesn't fall far from the tree"? This is true with any fruit, and it can apply to leaves. If the tree is planted on flat land, the fruit does not fall far. But what happens when a tree is planted on the peak of a hill or mountain? The fruit that falls from its branches is subject to be influenced by the force of gravity (a downward pulling) and roll away from the tree. If the wind is strong enough, it will aid with causing the fruit to move even farther from the tree. As it rolls it is subject to pick up all sorts of debris. And let us not forget the decaying process that soon follows. Don't get me wrong. Decay is good because through decay, life can begin again. But there is a big difference between fruit falling from a tree versus it being plucked from the tree. All of us should be allowing others to pluck life-giving fruit from our tree, but so often we give fruit that is already decaying. Like Christ, we must give good fruit. Some have collected fruit that has been infested with debris and has begun the process of decay. This means they are receiving corrupt fruit. In other words, they are giving themselves words that were not meant for them. Those that needed a word from God were too immature to digest the word. In our zeal to show how deep we are in spiritual things, we attempt to stuff them on words that they are not mature enough to receive. Because we are blind and have no discernment, we run them away.

You can pray this prayer daily. "Father God, help me to be the person you created me to be. Help me to mature into the spiritual adult that you envisioned me to be. Thank you for opening my eyes to my toddler way of looking at life, for helping me to see the condition of this world, what my life is without you, and the way I should be viewing my life in your."

Let us all pay attention to the fact that the seed we give is a seed that needs to germinate in the soil of the mind of the person who receives it. Make sure that seed is correct, timely, and holy. It is time to graduate from our toddler preschool mentality, move to first grade, and pursue our spiritual doctorate in the building of God's kingdom on earth. Amen!

CHAPTER 4
The Facts of Life

§

"In the beginning God created the heaven and the earth. And the earth was without form, and void; and darkness was upon the face of the deep. And the spirit of God moved upon the face of the waters" (*Gen. 1:1–2*).

WOULD YOU BELIEVE ME IF I said that a seed produces its own kind? This is how God constructed life to be. What happened between the "A" and "B" part of verse one is quite interesting. Could it be that between these two thoughts Satan (Lucifer) stepped into the picture and introduced chaos? Let's look at what *Isaiah 14:12–14* has to say:

> How art thou fallen from heaven O Lucifer son of the morning? How are thou cut down to the ground, who didst weaken the nations? For thou hast said in thine heart I will ascend into heaven, I will exalt my throne above the stars of God; I will set also upon the mount of the congregation, in the sides of the north, I will ascend above the heights of the clouds, I will be like the Most High.

It is mind-blowing how Satan has deceived the world into thinking he doesn't exist? Truth be told, he is the prince of this world system. He is the real unseen ruler of the ever-changing world powers. He is the daystar. The king of Babylon is Lucifer. There are several adjectives to describe the nature of Satan: persecutor, hater, destruction, attacker, accuser, and adversary, to list a few.

> *Fact*: Man's regal desire is to be like God.
> *Fact*: Man's greatest fear is that of rejection.
> *Fact*: Man's strongest lust is for self.

The knowledge man has obtained in the fields of medicine, science, and technology are astonishing—robotics, test-tube babies, frozen embryos, and don't forget the cell phone. Man has the ability to take a small chick and in a short time have it ready for slaughter; fryers are usually ready by six to eight weeks, broilers by six to eight weeks, and roasters less than 8 months.[1] Yes! We are living in the assumed perfect utopia, yet as we ever learn, we have forgotten how to submit to Him who created us. Just as important, we have forgotten what we are to subdue. Every imagination of man is in full bloom in this world today. What is so dangerous about this blooming is the fact that it leaves no room for God in it. Everything produced today has the overtone of being good for mankind, but the undertone is all about profit. Like toddlers, man's self-centeredness of discoveries and revelations are not kingdom of God-based. His motives are worldly and more destructive. In the military and in law enforcement, it is called collateral damage. You and I are to be forfeited in the event of default. Satan is saying, "Sin is the default. Man has forfeited his right to be called a son of God and now belongs to me." And what is our response to all of this? We, the church, in our attempt to be politically correct, have opened our arms and embraced it. We are now sleeping with the enemy.

> "Now the serpent was more subtle than any beast of the field which the Lord God had made. And he said unto the woman, Yea, hath God said, Ye shall not eat of every tree of the garden" (*Gen. 3:1*).

Satan is good at making use of clever and indirect methods to achieve his end—the destruction of man. Satan took God's words out of context and proclaimed it as truth, while Eve added to the contextual meaning of His word. Please note here that Satan is always attacking your mind garden. He knows your territory better than you do. He leaves the field of his domain and roams through your garden—the garden of your mind—and when you don't combat him with the Word of God, Satan will pounce on your ignorance every time. *Just because you may be mature in worldly things does not make you wise in the things of God.* This is where so many believers make their mistake. We want to combine our worldly knowledge with our limited spiritual knowledge and self-medicate ourselves into believing that God has ordained what we are doing. So many today in the body of Christ can talk good church ethics. They know scripture and they know the dynamics of the church structure—its programs, its language, and God's Word—but they are missing a committed relationship with Christ. Let me add that Satan too knows the dynamics of the church structure—its programs, its language, and God's Word—but he is missing a committed relationship to God as well. Like Satan, there are many who are not willing to submit their all to God. We are not all in.

Let us not forget that the majority of our lives have been lived in our flesh. It is only recently that some of us have come into a knowledge of God, and even with that knowledge, we have not built on it. The ability to submit seems to leave a sour taste in our mouths because so many of us want to be in charge of our own selves. Our ability to find fault with everyone and everything centers on our belief that nothing can work correctly unless we are in charge and those around us submit to our wishes. We seek the glory of men by taking, and fail to possess the glory of God by giving. When was the last time you put someone first—ahead of your wants and desires? When was the last time you submitted, surrendered your authority to someone other than yourself? When was the last time you willingly followed?

Everyone wants independence. If you have children, you know what I mean. While in their infant state, they are totally dependent on you as the parent. As they learn how to feed themselves, clean themselves, clean their rooms, and take limited responsibility for their assigned responsibilities around the house, they seek more and more independence to explore the outside world. I have yet to ask a child, "Who do you want to be like when you grow up?" and have him or her say, "A child of God." You cannot protect children from the outside world; be assured, they must go into it, bump their heads, and prayerfully find God. It is a fact of life. When the correct foundation is set in the home, they might take wisdom with them and develop the ability to make godly life choices.

Every child has his or her own temperament. No two children are the same. Like a fingerprint, each is different. It is interesting that as adults, we fail to accept this reality with one another. It is difficult for me to accept your difference in behavior, in opinion, in problem solving, in lifestyle, in dress, and so on, but I expect you to accept mine and to be supportive of my difference. This is why we must take the focus off ourselves and place our focus on Christ. Before we can come on one accord with one another, we must come on one accord with Him. It is our differences that make us unique. As a body of believers, we all have a function.

Let's use music as an example. The key to good music is the harmony that the different instruments and the vocalist make when each note is pitched and tuned correctly. This principle also applies to life. All of us should be planting the seeds of the love of God deep in the mind soil of all whom we meet. This planting enables us to mature into the perfect pitch and harmony of God. Satan wants to pit you against God, he wants to pit me against you, and he wants to pit you against me. He wants to change our pitch. He wants to pitch some too high so that pride will be their tone. He wants to pitch others low so that low self-esteem will be their tone. Satan wants to pit us against one another so that we will not be in harmony with God. This is called chaos, confusion and disorder. Stop here for a few minutes and read *Matthew 4:8–11*. There is a valuable lesson Jesus teaches us in this scripture. Like the media of today, Satan is always attempting to get us to look inwardly—self-pitch and outwardly – pride. There is a problem with the inside and outside of us, and Satan wants us to believe he has the answer to fix that specific problem. Somebody help me understand. How can the author of sin fix himself? He cannot and will not fight against his own kingdom. We fail to realize that to Satan, everything about us is a problem when we have sold out and are in pitch (perfect harmony) with Christ. When a soul is dedicated to Christ, it doesn't focus on itself internally or externally. Its whole focus is on "Thou shalt worship the Lord, thy God, and Him only shalt thou serve." Self never comes up for discussion.

When a soul is determined to make its own pitch, it sets a disturbing tone in the universe. That soul becomes noise and sets itself against the natural flow of God's designed harmony. *John 17:21* reads: "That all of them may be one, Father, just as you are in me and I am in you. May they also be in us so that the world may believe that you have sent me." Adam (man) was created in the image of God. He has emotions, feelings, and so on. But to deny the moral nature of God is how Satan has caused many to fall. When we choose to not honor God, we disrespect Him who created us; we disrespect our heavenly Father. When we disrespect Him, we swing open the door of chaos that Satan holds as a demonic gift for our soul. Take a few minutes and read *Ephesians 6:1–3* and then compare it with *Exodus 20:1–7*, and let us not forget *Matthew 4:4*. In our attempt as men to be independent, we have been cursed. Go back and read *verse 3* of *Ephesians 6*. How many of you are truly enjoying life here on earth?

All of us need to take some time to look within ourselves and find that pivotal moment, that core event that caused us to set our own pitch against the pitch of God. It could have been a parent, a friend, a teacher, a coworker, or a traumatic experiences at any developmental stage of our lives that caused us to lose our holy pitch. This is a fact. We were all born in sin and shaped in iniquity (*Ps. 51:5*). Satan thought that he had fixed the fight at Calvary, but he forgot who he was in the battle with. Now Satan is on the run. He knows he doesn't have much time left, and he has pulled out his whole arsenal against the sons of God. He knows he has lost, so he wants to repeat what he did with the heavenly host with man. He wants to take as many men, women, boys, and girls with him as will believe his lie.

Rejection

> "But unto Cain and to his offering He had not respect. And Cain was very wroth, and his countenance fell" (*Gen. 4:5*).

I have seen so many potential warriors for Christ stumble and fall because of rejection. Some rejection is warranted because of the carnal offering we present to God. This spiritual correction is from our God. There is another type of rejection that isn't warranted. It comes from the mind of someone's insecurity and fear of their anointing. This is carnal rejection. Carnal rejection can cause an individual to do some strange things. Rejection is an approach Satan uses to have an individual focus on himself or herself and not on God. This type of rejection gets people to focus on their wants, not their need of others, and because of this, they become self-centered, self-absorbed, self-distant, and self-destructive.

Every person wants to feel valued; however, too few have their value placed in the pitch of God. All of us are valued by God, but we fail to adhere to that value. We tend to seek the approval of others and work diligently to obtain their acceptance. Why do we seek the approval of those who have no power to put us in or take us out of heaven or hell? Could it be because we operate more on our feelings and emotions than in the spirit? Please note that God cursed man and the ground in *Genesis 3:17–19*. Because man chose to operate in his flesh, his dirt, this choice cursed his relationship with nature. Where we were to just gather fruit from the trees, we now have to work for it. The operative word here is work. After we receive salvation, God calls us to work. What should have been a natural behavior for us now has become a chore. Listing to Satan has made it difficult for some to pursue the things of God.

I have noted in raising children that they tend to place little emphasis on their action(s), resulting in a punishment. To them, the punishment tends to always outweigh what they did to obtain the punishment. After many years have gone by, they will remember the punishment and forget their actions that caused it. This one-sided core memory has caused great divides between parents and their offspring. But let the truth be told: adults have this same propensity for selective amnesia. We tend to remember what justifies us and discard that feeling of rejection. We fight against rejection by rejecting the truth that caused the rejection in the first place. Like Cain, I don't have to change my life when I justify my behavior predicated on my self-will. Who are you to tell me I am wrong?

Whereas rejection should cause us to examine ourselves in the Spirit of God's word, we tend to examine it in relation to our emotion and our feelings, earthly minded characteristics—our flesh. Remember now, the earth has been cursed. *You have to work by the sweat of your brow, and it still fails to yield good fruit for the mind.* Until we give the Holy Spirit dominion over our actions, thorns and thistles shall be the weeds taking root in our mind garden. Whenever an individual becomes self-governed, self-ruled, self-sufficient, self-reliant, and self-determined, that person's independent state of mind becomes separated from the needs of others and from the will of God. That person may no longer feels rejected; he or she becomes the rejecter. Rejection is a mind trait. It can only be conquered by a renewing of the mind.

The weeds of rejection are spawned when an individual's choice of action is carelessly and thoughtlessly offered, like Cain. God wants a life sacrificial offering like Abel. We have to examine ourselves to confirm if our sacrifice is worthy. Are we really sacrificing ourselves to God, or are we sacrificing stuff that is already dead to God? Our faithlessness toward God's ability to restore and raise us up out of the darkest sin in our lives keeps us from surrendering our total self to Him. Because we have rejected ourselves, we reject God. This is a trick of the devil, and today, you are going to put a stop to this lie.

LUST

Isn't it strange to you that when you first see or hear the word *lust,* you unconsciously think of sex? This is another weed that Satan has strategically planted in the garden of the mind. The Wikipedia encyclopedia's definition for lust is: "An emotion or feeling of intense desire in the body.

The lust can take any form such as the lust for knowledge, the lust for sex or the lust for power. It can take such mundane forms as the lust for food as distinct from the need for food. Lust is a psychological force producing intense wanting for an object, or circumstance fulfilling the emotion."[2]

This definition reminds me of the word *addiction*. *Addiction* is a state characterized by compulsive engagement in *reward stimuli* despite adverse consequences. It can be thought of as a disease or biological process leading to such behaviors. The two properties that characterize all addictive stimuli are that they are *reinforcing* (i.e., they increase the likelihood that a person will seek repeated exposure to them) and intrinsically rewarding (i.e., something perceived as being positive or desirable). Addiction is classified as a disorder of the brain's *reward system*, which arises through *transcriptional* and *epigenetic* mechanisms and occurs over time from chronically high levels of exposure to an addictive stimulus (e.g., morphine, cocaine, sexual intercourse, gambling, etc.).[3] Sin is a stimulus that attempts to override God's DNA in you to cause you to misread the call of God on your life; *it is the attempt to splice something that is natural and graft it onto the spiritual*.

Everyone is addicted to something or someone—your desire, your passion. It is what you lust for. The single woman wanting a husband, the fatherless child wanting a father, the person that lives in his or her own thoughts, the pursuit of knowledge—all can become lustful. All of these feelings, emotions, desires, and wants can become a type of lust, an addiction, if the person affected by them succumbs to their call. Satan has had a lot of time to develop methods that distract each of us from our purpose and our destiny. He already knows that you have the favor of God in your life, and he is counting on the distractions of life to keep you from reaching your full calling in God. Have you considered the *diversions* in your life? Have you considered the *agitations*? Have you noticed the *worriers* that keep you from the high calling of God on your life? Please note that they all are temporal, they are earthly, and they are fleshly. Answer this question: What diversions, what agitations, and what worriers do you have in the spirit? Your answer will always be *none*.

More Christians need to lust more for the things of God. More Christians need to be addicted to the things of God. *1 Corinthians 16:15* reads: "I beseech you brethren, ye know the house of Stephanan, that it is the first fruits of Achia (Greece), and that they have *addicted* themselves to the ministry of the saints." Stephanan's house is a challenge to all of us. He was a Greek—a pagan like you and I—who became a follower of Christ and lived to minister to the saints. He had only one lust—a lust to please God. His lust and his addiction were *spiritual*. His life ambition was to please God and honor Him through his service to the saints. What a witness to us in the twenty-first century. The house of Stephanan was very willing to suffer the rejection of their kinsmen for the furtherance of the gospel of Christ. As the churches around the world, even in North America, are being persecuted by their governments, we all need to pray for each believer to die to themselves, reject everything that is not Christ-centered, and become addicted for the desires of God's heart, not their own.

I strongly urge you to take a few minutes right now and ask God, in the name of Jesus, to reveal to you those areas of your life that you have kept for yourself and have not given to Him. Those areas of rejection and the different lusts in your life that have grown into weeds and have separated you from God and from those souls that He has called you to minister to. If you would just slow down for a few minutes and listen to His voice inside of your mind garden, you would begin to gain your focus. You would begin to move out of the darkness of your past hurts and disappointments and move in the healing light of God's love for you. You can do it. God believes in you, and so do I. He is waiting right now to give life to you and that more abundantly. That is the fact of life.

CHAPTER 5
Dirt in Your I

As a surgeon is willing to cut into a body through the bone and actually remove, examine, and chart the organs that lie within the human body, this chapter is here to cut through the spirit of man and actually remove, examine, and chart for you those satanical weeds that have taken strong root in the garden of your mind.

After the examination has taken place, it becomes your responsibility to root them out of your mind and out of your life. You will need to make time to study God's word and attach yourself to someone who can guide you into your deliverance. God already has that person ready to receive you. None of us are really who we think we are. What we are, however, is a mixture of life experiences—some good, some not so good. Our lives have been touched by our parents, our grandparents, our friends, our teachers, our playmates, our classmates, and so on. All of the above and more have played a part in making us who we are today and in the establishment of our character. Their conversations with us and their actions around us have played an integral part in how we think, how we act, and how we feel about ourselves, others, and this world we live in.

With the instant replay button turned on in our thinking, we can begin looking at spiritual truth through skewed lenses and totally not see God. All of us must be cognizant of this fact: The kingdom of darkness is seeking your attention and it is the loudest voice in the garden of your mind, *your thoughts*. Few people pay attention to their thoughts. I call it *mind talk*. You know, when someone does something to you, be it good or bad, you talk to yourself about it. You literally discuss how you feel and how you want to respond to the act. If you don't act on your feeling then, you store it in your core memory, and each time you see that person, you relive the event and negative images you created toward that person. Those images take root in your mind, and before you know it, that person has become dead to you.

Your spirit man is the aspect of your humanity that should connect with God. We have a spirit, we are a soul, and we live in *dirt*. Your dirt seeks only immediate satisfaction. The soul is in constant interaction with your dirt. Just as we inherit the genes of our parents and learn from the behaviors of those whom we observe, our spirit inherits everything that our physical body does. We can't take money, fame, or anything physical with us after we die, but our spirit inherits the attitudes, tendencies, character, and mentality with which our dirt lived.

In religious terms, our spirit will possess either a sin nature or a godlike nature depending on how we choose to live our physical life. *How you live your physical life will determine your spiritual fate. Your thoughts become actions, your actions become habits, your habits become your character, and your character determines your fate. As you think, so you become.*

"There is a natural body, and there is also a spiritual body." (*1 Cor. 15:44b*).

Just as surely as you have a physical body that lives in the physical world, you also have a spiritual body that lives in the spiritual world.

Just as there is both male and female, there is also both physical and spiritual. While you are physically alive in this world, your body, your soul, and your spirit are all connected. Let me say it in another way. Your spiritual body inherits everything that your physical body does. You can't take money, fame, or anything physical with you after you die but your spirit inherits the attitudes, tendencies, character, and mentality with which your body lived.

If you regularly take action on the word of God, take joy in honoring God through expressions of love, and grow into a loving relationship with God, then your spirit will grow strong and healthy and experience a loving relationship with all who come into your life's experiences. You will become sensitive to the needs of all with whom you come into contact. This is the nature that Jesus possessed as He taught repentance. But if you live only to satisfy physical desires, then your spirit will suffer from malnourishment and easily succumb to selfish, hateful, or wicked influences. You negatively impact the garden of your mind; you hate those around you, and you hate God. You then are subject to become pure evil.

Having a spirit is what separates us from animals. It is our spirit that lives forever, and it desires to know about and connect with God in the spiritual world. It is our spirit that desires to be holy and to see good done for others. It is our spirit that is righteous or wicked, and ultimately it is our spirit that goes to either heaven or hell.

> "Verily I say unto you, whatever you bind on earth will be bound in heaven, and whatever you loose on earth will be loosed in heaven" (*Matthew 18:18*).

Many people ignore the spiritual world. Or even if they believe in life after death, people live thinking that there is no way to know what will happen after you die. But actually we can know very well and should know what to expect because *the purpose of your life here on this earth is to prepare you for eternal life with God.*

So, no one after today can say that he or she doesn't know what his or her purpose is. Your purpose is to know and love God, to enter into a loving fellowship with Him and all of mankind. As you feed daily on the word of God, you begin to shift from carnal to spiritual. As you begin to shift from carnal to spiritual, your flesh begins to die, and your spirit man becomes alive; it begins to thirst for God, and you begin to put the needs of others before your wants. As your flesh begins to die and your spirit man becomes alive, your life begins to impact the lives of those with whom you come into contact. Just like with Christ, they will both love you and seek to become like Christ, or they will hate you and attempt to destroy the Christ in you. You move from trying to please the world to a loving relationship with God that takes you into His presence.

Throughout history there have been countless accounts of people going to the spiritual world and telling firsthand what they experienced. Some people are very spiritual and able to tell us what their spirits see in the spiritual world. Others have tapped into the wrong spiritual realm and have allowed the wrong type of spirits to enter into the earth realm. We tend to not accept this fact even though it has been recorded in both the Old and New Testament. At the end of this chapter, please take time to look at *Ephesians 5:8, Galatians 5:16–25, 1 John 2:6,* and *Colossians 3:16.* The only way to walk in the word of God is to become the word of God. You are what you eat.

> "And Jacob called the name of the place Peniel; for I have seen God face to face, and my life is preserved" (*Gen. 32:30*).

Listen to what Jesus says in *Matthew 6:22*: "The light (lamp) of the body is the eye; if, therefore, thine eye be single (healthy), the whole body shall be full of light."

Now read *1 John 1:5*: "This then is the message which we have heard of Him, and declare unto you, that God is light, and in him is no darkness at all."

And read *1 Timothy 6:16*: "Who only have immortality, dwelling in the light which no man can approach unto; whom no man hath seen, nor can see to whom be honor and power everlasting, Amen."

I can't answer for you, but I want my eyes opened fully to the glory of God and not to the chaos of this dying world. But I have to get past the darkness in me in order to obtain my sight. My flesh can't see nor can it approach God. Only my spirit man can. If I do not allow the light of God, the light of Christ, and the light of the Holy Spirit to shine into my darkness and illuminate my sight, I will not be full of light, which means I will not be full of the righteousness of God. *1 Corinthians 13:12* reads: "For now we see through a glass, darkly; but then face to face: I know even as also I am known." How do you see yourself? How do the people in your line of influence see you? How does your family see you? Our tendency to see ourselves differently than those around us is commonplace. This is why many of us tend to wonder why we are not liked by all.

While in the military as a training instructor, I wanted to be liked by everyone I came into contact with. One day I found myself fighting with myself over those individuals who did not like me. My commanding officer called me into his office to discuss the distress I was feeling. Even though he was not the most religious man I had met, he gave me some advice that impacted me for the rest of my life. He said, "You can walk in a room that has one hundred people in it. Half of them will like you, and the other half of them will not simply on how they perceived you when you entered the room." I know I'm not perfect, and I know God through the Holy Spirit is working on me. If I know all of this, why was I allowing other people to influence how I feel about me? As a child I heard so many negative things said to me about my looks, about my thinking, and about my abilities that I somewhat began to internalize them as real. Even though I was saved, the thoughts and images haunted me. After that meeting with my commanding officer, I realized that I'm a work in progress. God's hand is on my life and I am favored by God.

Worlds

Let us revisit what I brought up in chapter 1 about external and internal worlds. We live in two worlds. The first world is the one that we move through; we talk to people and have interactions with them. This is the natural world. The second world is between our ears—our mind. Both worlds are feeding off each other. As with all of us, our core inward thoughts and feelings about ourselves can be influenced by the external images we accept from the external and the internal images we believe about ourselves. When a person operates out of a desire to be accepted by the influence of the world, he or she is subject to have a world view of how things are and how things should be.

Let me state here again, this earth has been cursed, which means your flesh is cursed. So as your flesh is cursed, so goes your carnal thinking. As this earth yields weeds, so does the flesh. Did you know that weeds come in the colors of the rainbow just like flowers? But their roots take up all the soil from the plants that are good. If a person fills his or her life with the flashy colors of this external world and lives in the internal world individually in his or her mind, those worlds will take over the fertile spiritual ground of the word of God and replace it with a destructive life nature— the powers of darkness. Remember, as God's Spirit moved on the darkness that was upon the face of the deep, God said, "Let there be light." Your light today is the word of God, the truth of your existence.

God's Spirit is always moving over the dark areas in your life seeking to speak light and life into your situation. Each of us must see the light of God working in our situation, in our circumstances. His Spirit is always looking to bring light to our dark places, and trust me, we all have them. God does this by spiritually tilling and plowing our mind soul. He seeks to remove the pebbles, the rocks, the stones, and the weeds from our mind garden so that He can rain on our soil the good news of the gospel of Christ—so that He can irrigate our minds to receive the pure word of the gospel. He wants to shine the light of His truth onto us so that we may mature and be fruitful for His kingdom.

Tilling our carnal soul is painful. There are so many dead things in us that we have become accustomed to, addicted to, and lust for; we feel that we cannot live without them. We own them. We hoard them. Think about it for one minute. Everything about you right now is centered on satisfying you, somebody else and not on satisfying God's will for your life. Now take a few minutes more and think about that person that your best friend told you he or she didn't like. So now you don't like that person, even though you don't know him or her. You chose to not like the person because your friend doesn't like them. Because of the negative feelings your friend has for the person, you forgo the opportunity to witness to either of them the love of Christ. This is one area where Satan has been effective in planting weeds—weeds of discord, weeds of indifference, weeds of hate, and weeds of death. Each of our lives are to be lived in the pursuit of bringing the life of Christ to everyone we have opportunity to witness to. No one is excluded. When our friends talk negatively about someone, speaking death, it is our responsibility to speak life. We should never speak death into the life of anyone.

Moses was placed in a cleft of a rock (*Exod. 33:22-23*). Now read *1 Corinthians 13:12*. Moses, like us, cannot fathom the awesomeness of God. We cannot take in all that God is in one setting. We need to receive it in consumable pieces. A child starts out on milk. From milk the child moves to shredded foods that are digestible in his or her tender stomach. As the child matures, he or she can consume more solid foods; however, it would not be wise for us to stuff our infant with solid foods, for we would cause the infant to choke. God feeds us at the level we are spiritually capable of consuming His word. Too often, however, the novice takes a little bit of the world, refuses to come back to the table, and attempts to feed others the little bit he or she has. After exhausting his or her portion, the novice has nothing left to sustain him or her for the next attack of the enemy. The novice finds himself or herself in a weakened state. In that weakened state, the novice begins to demand more than he or she can digest and begins to regurgitate the excess, or the novice begins to feed on the lies of Satan.

Such a novice took a little and attempted to make much out of it. Now he or she is embarrassed and feels like a castaway. The novice feels like he or she doesn't fit in because he or she sees how selfish and possessive he or she was with the word of God. His or her speech revealed how self-centered he or she was regarding the little bit of the world he or she received. The novice failed to digest the word but regurgitated it out of his or her spirit man. The novice now sees how inadequate he or she is in the use of the word of God. Like Moses, he or she must now seek a new and clearer vision from God. God wants to show us His glory. We cannot receive it all at once, so God puts us in the cleft of the rock—the cleft of Jesus. Here in the cleft of the rock, the open and scared areas of our life, Jesus gives us no more than what we can bear. He covers us with His blood as He passes by so we can heal from the battles lost in our own attempts to fight Satan.

God wants to take us from being dirt to being a rock. But not just any rock. We too have the awesome responsibility to cover the sins of all whom we come into contact with. Like God covered Moses with His hand and how Christ covers us in His blood, we are to cover one another with the love of God and prayer. This is our rock. When we take the focus off ourselves, we will be able to see the spiritual need of those around us. And in seeing their need, *you* begin to supply that need through the power of Christ Jesus in you and the gift that He has given you.

Yes! We are dirt, but we are more than that. We have been created in the image of God. We must put off the spirit of Satan, the spirit to kill, the spirit to still, and the spirit to destroy one another. We were once damaged fruit, but the Spirit of God now lives in us, showing us how to be producers of good fruit. Let us live in this world, our flesh, and bear, birth, and produce fruit fit for the kingdom of God. Yes, we can! Each of us has been bought with a price. We must recognize that we are passing through time on our way to eternity with our heavenly Father. It is my hope and prayer that you will be willing to pay the price to keep your spiritual freedom. You are now gainfully employd for kingdom building with a retirement plan that is out of this world. When you get the dirt out of your I, the light of God will shine in and overtake the dirty and dark areas of your life. Walk fully in His light. Just lie on the spiritual surgical table of God, and He will remove the spiritual weeds that have infected you and taken strong root in the garden of your mind. His light will remove all shadows from your thinking. There will be no more hidden places for Satan in the mind garden of your mind, and the dirt will be removed from your I.

Pray this prayer: "Today Lord, in the mighty name of Jesus, I will become violent for the things of God, for the pulling down of strongholds and for the perfecting of the Saints. I chose today to gather the redeemed from the hands of the enemy. I will guide them out of their wilderness of unrest so that my God may give them a spirit of praise. My God is wise and able to accomplish what He speaks. I will praise you God with my whole heart. I will be a temple of worship in your name. You have searched me and know me O my God and I surrender all of my thoughts and my imaginations to your will. Have your way with me my God for you are completing a perfect work in me. You are my savior and you are my LORD and I proclaim this day, no more dirt in my I."

CHAPTER 6
Wayward Instructions

§

Hear ye this, O priests; and hearken, ye house of the king; for judgment is toward you, because ye have been a snare on Mizpah, and a net spread upon Tabor.

And the revolters are profound to make slaughter, though I have been a rebuke of them all.

I know Ephraim, and Israel is not hidden from me: for now, O Ephraim, thou committest whoredom, and Israel is defiled.

They will not frame their doings to turn unto their God: for the spirit of whoredom is in the midst of them, and they have not known the Lord.

And the pride of Israel doth testify to his face; therefore shall Israel and Ephraim fall in their iniquity; Judah also shall fall with them.

They shall go with their flocks and with their herds to seek the Lord, but they shall not find him; he hath withdrawn himself from them.

They have dealt treacherously against the Lord; *for they have begotten strange children*; now shall a moth devour them with their portions (*Hosea 5:1–7*).

GOD WANTS TO TALK TO parents today. Many parents are concerned with the decay of the family structure and the maturing of more violence in the world but have failed to realize that they are the key to its turnaround.

Regardless of economic status, everyone is increasingly becoming aware that there is something wrong globally. You would think that with so many churches in Christian and Jewish religious affiliates around the world, things would be getting better, not worse. But this is not the case.

Just like in the day of Hosea, our present-day priests and kings are being judged because they have become a snare to the children. In the year 2015, who are the priests and kings God is talking about? The answer to that question is "you." All parents, guardians, those responsible for the welfare of children and all who spend any time with children are the present-day priests and kings. So why are we being judged?

We cuss, we lie, and we have our children lie for us. We talk about people, we belittle people, and we put *things* before God and his children—all in an attempt to be successful and to be recognized by our peers. Our children don't see us reading and studying our Bible. They don't see us praying. We don't eat together or study the Word of God together. We don't even make it a priority for the *family* to pray together, not even for a few minutes, nor to spend time together daily seeking God's presence and direction for the purpose of the family. *We have lost our witness.* We're in church, but we don't know Christ. We have become like Lot. The children of today are telling their parents what they will and will not do.

When was the last time your family had a revival, not within the confines of the church you attend, but within the confines of your home? When was the last time your family went on a retreat, withdrew from the affairs of this life, and took time away together to seek the presence of God? In today's world, we are so busy doing worldly things that any activity that has God attached to it is limited to two days per week for a total of four hours—*Sunday* two hours and *midweek Bible study* two hours. And that only holds true if we feel like it. Each parent and guardian today is to be a Mizpah in his or her home, a *watchtower*. It is our responsibility to watch over the souls of our children day and night until they reach the age of accountability. And even after that we are required to give sound biblical counsel to mature their faith.

Parents are to be spiritual bouncers over the souls of their children. Think of your child's emotions and feelings as a campground. This is where your family camps out night after night. Satan camps there too. Someone has to stand guard at night and in the day. Activity is always going on, but there are some activities that should not be allowed into the camp. As parents, guardians, and protectors, we stand at the door of our children's minds; we are the *gatekeeper* for the things that present themselves as worthy of entry into the emotional realm of our children's minds. Our first responsibility to our children is to build a trusting relationship with them, a foundation in God's word. We must keep the door open for our children to talk to us about anything. We are to command our emotions so as to not present gestures of rejection of their thinking and feeling on what they think and feel. Our role is to always have spiritual dialogue with them so that we can guide them in what God says about an issue—not our opinion. Remember, everything about your home should be a place of protection felt by each family member.

It is also our responsibility to sound the alarm when Satan seeks to enter the camp of our home and the minds of our children. Satan is always attempting to place us in bondage to the things of this world and the negative things of our past. But we should also be the Tabor, *the high place* in our home, and should possess the ability, with a panoramic view of our children's emotional, physical, and spiritual condition, to see the works of Satan. We should place a spiritual hedge of protection around their souls and the souls of all of our family members. In this scripture, however, God is saying we have become the snare in our children's lives. God is saying we have become the net that is keeping them from spiritual flight and keeping them in Babylon—the earth realm. If this is you, what do you think you need to do right now to effect a change? There is a way that seems right to us, but if we are not careful, we may be the cause of the spiritual death of our children. We must be willing to listen before we speak and really hear what our children's emotions are—not what we want them to be. We must learn how, through the word of God, to take them from where they are, in love, and gently guide them to where God wants them to be, not where we want them to be.

> "Be sober, be vigilant, because your adversary, the devil, like a roaring lion walked about, seeking whom he may devour" (*1 Pet. 5:8*).

Each and every one of us has an adversary. Each and every one of us is tasked to be sober, yet many are drunk with desires to have more of what this world has, and this causes them to have less of God and what He wants in their lives. We seek more physical prosperity and little spiritual prosperity. We seek more financial wealth but are broke in faith. We like to give our testimony on praise and worship but are in a drought when it comes to prayer and fasting.

We are tasked to be vigilant, but we are not vigilant for the things of the kingdom of God. We are, however, vigilant for the things of this world. Across America, the average born-again believer is not involved in any kingdom-building ministries in his or her local church. *People come to church, sit in the pew, praise the Lord, and go home.* They have disengaged themselves from the call of God on their lives. Many don't even know what their godly calling is. This can be seen clearly in the male population of the church. They can talk about sports, their cars, their job titles, their positions in life, their children, and even their church and pastor, but to make it a point to center all conversations on Christ is a little too much. We don't want to be looked upon as Jesus freaks. We just want to fit in. We call it balance. So many are not walking in the Spirit but are claiming its rewards. Could it be because in today's church we are seeking more physical and personal wealth and not the wealth of the kingdom of God? If you sought after the rich things of God, you would have the rich things of this earth. Jesus said in *Matthew 6:21*: "For where your treasure is, there will your heart be also." Too many have made themselves the treasure, not Christ.

At the close of this chapter, I want you to read *Genesis 15:1*. Right now God wants to birth offspring in you that follow Him. What hinders most of us from accepting the power of God to accomplish this is we focus on our failures, not on His favor in our lives. He has always been there waiting for us to submit to His will. He wants to bless us so much, but we must be worthy of the blessing. Just remember this: You too are a child. Like Abram and like all children, we don't understand clearly what our parents are attempting to teach us, but if we become obedient to their instructions, we will reap all the rewards of their favor. God favors us; *we must favor Him.*

> "For all that is in the world, the lust of the flesh, and the lust of the eyes, and the pride of life, is not of the father but are of the world" (*1 John 2:16*).

It is easy for us to blame our children for what is going on in their social environment—violence, drugs, selfies, the misrepresentation of women in their music, the explosion of sexual activity. It is easy for us to blame government, be it global, national, state, or local. We have even gone as far as to accept homosexuality as OK because we want to be politically correct and not infringe on the human (carnal) rights of others. It took the gay rights movement forty years to get legislators to approve their agenda. So now guess what's coming next?

As the commonality of the homosexual lifestyle is accepted, our children, some Christian, mind you, will look at it as normal, natural, and even healthy. And since that lifestyle is OK, bestiality is the next move of Satan in the garden of the minds of this generation.

Recently someone put on Facebook a short video of a young woman kissing her dog. This wasn't a person letting a pet lick her face. She held the dog's tongue in her mouth. Just before I witnessed that video, there was a report in the news of a man taking sexual advantage of a female puppy, resulting in the puppy becoming overly aggressive. Someone in the not too distant future is going to want to marry his or her pet. Why not? Your pet does what you want it to do when you want it to do it. For those who treat their pets like family members—they are a pet parent—the door for greater abominations to take place is on the horizon. Read *Leviticus 18:23–30*.

We can't get along today with one another because we want every person to do exactly want we want them to do—with *no questions asked.*

Why are we doing this? It is because when people don't have a God-centered life, they create their own god, and that god tends to be a reflection of themselves. God calls it idolatry. Ask Eve. Parents, we cannot teach our children anything related to the kingdom-building process until we are ready to get naked and stay naked before God. *It is all about the flesh.* All of us must confront our mistakes, confront our shortcomings, confront our failures, and yes, even confront the carnal things we lust for. After we confront them, we must repent and ask God to wash us in the blood of Christ. This is one of the reasons the Apostle Paul tells us in *Hebrews 10:25*, "Not forsaking the assembling of ourselves together, as the manner of some is; but exhorting one another: and so much the more, as ye see the day approaching." All confessing Christians need to have someone in their lives that will hold them accountable—a mature Christian that they can trust with their feelings and emotions. Narcotics Anonymous (NA) members come together daily and talk about their feelings and emotions and their progess with their addiction. When they talk about it to others, they are not judged but are encouraged to "keep coming back". This lets the person know that there will always be someone available to listen to them. Too many of the saints are living independent of the body of Christ, and like a severed finger, the longer they are away from the body, they will wither, shrivel, dry up, and die.

Why do I say this? I say it because each of us is responsible for planting spiritual seeds in the lives of all whom we come in contact with. If a carnal organization like NA can encourage its members, how much more should a spiritual organization like the church be able to encourage its members? *1 Corinthians 3:6* reads: "I have planted, Apollos watered; but God gave the increase." This scripture lets us see that even then, the church had started to move into denominationalism. The church in Corinth was moving not only toward independence, severing itself; but more importantly, the church began to feel a need to save itself from others believers so it began to separate from the body of Christ and developed external sects. We see these traits in the body of Christ today. If your pastor isn't preaching on a given Sunday, you don't show up. You have heard it said, "My church, my pastor," and so on. You don't hear it being said, "Boy, God sure used so-and-so today" and "Just give God the glory."

Like Israel, Christ's bride, the church, seems to seek after a leader whom they can see and touch. She doesn't want to hear the voice of the bridegroom because it means she has to submit to His authority. She only wants Him when she finds herself in trouble or when she wants something in the natural. It's like the couple who has been married over twenty years, and in some cases for a shorter time. She stays in the marriage for the financial support. He stays in the marriage because it's cheaper to keep her. They have become independent of each other and have not become one. But their church members are clueless because of the façade both of them cloth themselves in. This couple has learned quickly how to put on their church faces when they are out in public, but their mind garden is full of weeds of bitterness toward each other.

Who knows when they stopped planting? Who knows when they stopped watering? Here is a fact: God will always give the increase. What am I saying? Whatever situation, whatever circumstance, whatever trial or tribulation people find themselves in, they must make sure to keep God in it for He is the only one who can lead them out of it. He will lead us, He will walk beside us, and He will carry us. When we become separated from God, when we independently attempt to make it on our own, we become a severed member of His body, we become separated from the life-sustaining branch—Christ—and we wither. But thank God for the precious blood of Christ, which washes us and makes us new. This blood smooths out our wrinkles and cleanses all our spots and blemishes. Jesus is always sending spiritual seed for us to feed on; He is always watering the dried areas of our lives with a fresh anointing. But too many reject this water, for to drink it, we must see ourselves as we really are and see Christ as our Lord. It is one thing to see Him as your Savior; it is another thing altogether to see Him as your Savior and your Lord.

How do we begin the process of removing the weeds of this world from the garden of our mind so that we make Him Savior and Lord?

Before you retire to your bed tonight, get your family together and talk about the dysfunctions you have. Be honest!

Begin to pray with and for one another.

Start a daily family Bible study.

Eat a meal with the whole family and discuss what went on in your day.

Make the decision to put that cell phone down, cut that television off, and pick up your family.

Trust me, in time, you'll see the hand of God move. Revival will take place in your home, and you and your family will be effective witnesses of the glory of God in your life and your family's life. Your example will impact lives in your neighborhood and eventually in your church. Then, when someone asks you *"Why?"* you'll have the wisdom to lead that person to Christ. The instructions that such people received in their past that were wayward will be removed as God moves you from you and into Him.

CHAPTER 7
A Change of Heart

Then he said unto me, Son of Man, these bones are the whole house of Israel; behold, they say, Our bones are dried, and our hope is lost; we are cut off from our inheritance.

Therefore, prophesy and say unto them, thus saith the Lord God: Behold, O my people, I will open your graves, and cause you to come up out of your graves, and bring you into the land of Israel.

And ye shall know that I am the Lord, I have opened your graves, O my people, and brought you up out of your graves.

And shall put my Spirit in you, and ye shall live, and I shall place you in your own land; then shall ye know that I, the Lord, have spoken it, and performed it, saith the Lord *(Ezek. 37:11-14).*

THERE ARE SEVERAL WORDS AND statements God makes in these passages of scripture that I want you to underline.

- Our bones are dried.
- I will open your graves and…bring you into the land of Israel.
- I am.
- And shall put my Spirit in you.

Just as God has declared that He will put His Spirit in Israel, we as Christians should get excited. As adopted children, we too need His Spirit in us. But the question for today is, how did we lose His Spirit? For the answer let's go back to the garden.

What do you think when I say, "We are the fruit of God, but many of us are rotten fruit?" Let me explain. *Genesis 2:15* says, "And the Lord God took the man and put (planted) him into the Garden of Eden to dress it and to keep it." Now *envision God as the gardener.*

The "A" part of *Psalms 144:12* reads: "That our sons may be like plants grown up in their youth."

Matthew 13:24–25 reads: "Another parable put he forth unto them saying, 'The kingdom of heaven is likened unto a man who sowed good seed in his field: But, while men slept, his enemy came and sowed tares among the wheat, and went his way.'"

Matthew 15:13 reads: "But he answered and said, 'Every plant, which my heavenly Father hath not planted, shall be rooted up.'"

Church, our purpose in the Garden of Eden was to dress the garden with the seeds God gave us. Like fruit trees, we were to produce seed after our own kind—the image of God—and fill the earth with it. But something happened. While we slept, this allowed Satan to come into God's garden—our mind—and plant tares. God said, "Be fruitful and multiply." Satan said, "Be like gods," and with our listening to Satan and not to God, that caused us to reproduce sin—and how it has multiplied on the earth!

I want you to capture this. The seeds from wheat are heavy and full. These seeds are at the top of the stalk, and like wheat, we should be top-heavy with the ministry of the gospel—the good news of Christ. Wheat looks very different when fully matured. *The operative words here are "fully matured."* Let me explain. Even though Adam and Eve were created with the ability to reproduce and name everything on the planet, they were not fully matured spiritually. They had not matured enough to handle evil. This is why God forbade them from taking of the fruit of the tree of the knowledge of good and evil. Even though we are saved, sanctified, and filled with the Holy Ghost, if we are honest with ourselves, there are areas in our lives that we still struggle with. Peter told Jesus that he would never deny Him, but Jesus had to tell him, "Verily I say unto thee, that this night, before the rooster (cock) crow, thou shalt deny me thrice (three times)" (Matt. 26:34). Just like Peter, there are many who are in denial. Yes, they love God, but when it is their turn to be sacrificed by this world for their obedience to His Word, they will deny Him.

When the winds of suffering come into some people's lives, they don't bend; they break. They break mentally and emotionally. Instead of giving their issues to God and leaving them there, they carry this baggage with them, which allows Satan to make their issues seem far worse than what they really are. Because they are unwilling to *give* their issues to God, Satan adds more issues. They take their eyes off God's ability to deliver, and they focus on their inability. When we focus all our energy on ourselves, we become stiff-necked; and when we become stiff-necked, it becomes easier for us to break.

Are You Wheat?

Wheat bows to the wind. Therefore when you see wheat at its peak and ready for harvest, it is bent according to which way the wind blew. Like wheat, when we are full with the breath of God, the Holy Spirit in our mind, He causes us to stay on *bended* knees. We spend time with the Lord and obey His word to the letter. We have no other desire because the seeds that are planted in us by Him are too strong and mighty in the word of God to stand upright with pride. This causes us to continuously bow in praise and worship to the God of our salvation. We also are able to bend under the pressures of life. We bend, but we don't break because God has our back. He is our support through our trials and tribulations in this life.

However, the tares are prideful and boastful. They are stubborn, reprobated, and self-endowed. They act like wheat, *but get this, people!* If you eat the seeds from the tare (Satan's seeds), they cause severe nausea and produce vomiting, severe headaches, and a host of other illnesses. We cannot operate like Eve, who listened to Satan; we cannot operate like Adam, who listened to Eve. We must be very careful of who we allow to speak and plant in our mind's garden. Our lives are a mixture of life experiences—some good and some not so good. Our inner lives have been touched by our parents, our grandparents, our cousins, our aunts and uncles, our friends, our playmates, our teachers, our classmates, and even our enemies. This is why we must weed out the bad influences of this world from the garden of our minds. Just as God gives us core memories of His life-giving goodness, Satan sends a counterfeit core memory of death and destruction.

Are You a Tare?

The tare's job is to choke the life out of the wheat and replace it in appearance. Satan's job is to choke the life out of you. Didn't God say, "for in the day that thou eatest there of thou shall surely die"? Note this: Tares are smaller than wheat and more easily swallowed. When they pass through our spiritual throat into our spiritual stomach, we stop talking like Christ. When we absorb them into our spiritual stomachs, like emboli, they infect every part of our spirit man. Let's face it: Sin is a disease that is infectious and an addictive killer that causes our spiritual bones to become dry. Because Adam and Eve had not yet built up a resistance, an immunity to evil, God warned them of its addictive consequences—death and spiritual separation.

What do you consume daily in your mind thought? You know! That time that you spend in yourself thinking that you are thinking about self-stuff, the truth is you are receiving death seed from Satan or life-giving seed from God into your mind.

Some of us, like Eve, sit next to, talk to, entertain, or are entertained by people like Satan. We do this in church, at home, and in the workplace and are totally unaware. We are unaware because we don't internalize the Word of God enough to know the difference. This is the reason for many of us having dry bones. We are in church, but we are dead and disconnected from the things of God. So many are choking and coughing when the truth is preached. When the Spirit of God speaks, many develop spiritual diarrhea and pass that word right out of their spirit. When we make up our mind to study God's Word, we get a spiritual headache, we get spiritually sleepy, and this causes us to focus on our natural condition and not on our spiritual condition. The spiritual you is *dead and buried in this earth—your flesh!* It needs a change; it needs to be revived and it needs deliverance.

Church, we need to understand that we can do nothing for Christ, in Christ, or through Christ unless the Father draws us. Jesus tells us in *John 6:44*: "No man can come to me except the Father, who hath sent me draw him; and I will raise him up at the last day."

Acts 2:17 says: "And it shall come to pass in the last days, saith God, I will pour out of my Spirit upon all flesh; and your sons and your daughters shall prophesy, and your young men shall see visions, and your old men shall dream dreams."

You see, if God doesn't draw you, call you out, and seek you, you *are* lost. *Question:* Is everyone who goes to church saved? *Question:* Is everyone who calls themselves Christian born again? The answer is a resounding *no* to both questions. However, your job is to be an effective example, an effective witness, and have the ability to discern the needs of the body of Christ in accordance to the gifts you are spiritually born with.

As we are in the last days—plural, mind you—God wants to take you out of your grave. Although many are dead to Him in their sins and dead to Him in their spirit, He loves each of us so much that He looks past our shortcomings and seeks to restore us to our beginning. Your first love! *Revelations 2:4.* The Ephesians realized that God loved them and had showed them their sinful state. Because God loves you so much, He should be your first love. He and only He should be the person that you live to please in love.

He wants to place His Spirit in you and place you back in His garden. It is crucial that we don't forget that this earth is not our home. We must become a prepared people for a prepared place. In *John 14:2* Jesus says that He is preparing a place for us, but so many see no future for themselves after the grave and believe that there is no life after the grave.

Restoration

Please hear me. As God's plan is to restore Israel, He also wants to restore you. But this will not happen unless you hear Him speak. Ezekiel was commanded to speak to the dry bones. I today am speaking to your dry bones. In the natural, your heart pumps blood through your body. This blood flow through your bone marrow, and without this blood, your bones become dry. It is the same for your spirit man. The blood of Christ is life for your spiritual bones.

When you put too much stock in your flesh and not God, it becomes hard to accept the fact that *your flesh is your biggest enemy.* Man was formed, made, created from dirt. Know this, church, God is not coming back for your dirt (your flesh); He is coming back for the fruit He planted in you. Today many have surrendered their lives to their flesh, and their flesh dictates to their soul, their soul dictates to their spirit, and their spirit has become lost (dead). This should not be the case. God's original design was for His Spirit to instruct our spirit, our spirit to instruct our soul, and our soul to instruct our flesh. Too many of us are allowing this process to operate in reverse: our flesh is instructing our soul, and our soul is instructing our spirit. This is because we have made our flesh more important than our spirit.

We must bring each thought under the microscope of God. Please note that you have lived longer with your flesh than with God, but your flesh represents death and God's spirit represents life. Choose this day whom you will serve. Jesus stated that He is preparing a place for us. I would venture to say that there is a land waiting for each of us to take residence, a land waiting for us to inherit. As with a bride who takes residence in her husband, we are to take residence in Christ. We are to become *one* with Him as He is *one* with His Father.

There is someone right now who is reading this chapter who has an area in your life that is closed off from God. You have been hurt and dismembered from a free and fruitful life in Christ. *You have allowed what people have said and done to you in the physical past to negatively impact your spiritual future.* You have spiritually dried up and died. You are walking in a spiritual grave and cannot adhere to the things of God because you have been bombarded with so many dead things in your life. Even as a child, you struggled with being accepted, you didn't fit in, and you were an outcast. Let me tell you right now that the reason for those emotions is that God has something better for you. He wants to draw you away from the words of this world. Satan's army is working very hard to keep you from seeing how your God-saving testimony is a soul-winning witness in other people's lives. You are a fruit barrier and Satan doesn't want you to produce fruit for God.

Today God is saying that He will open your grave and cause you to come up out of your grave. He will bring you into the land of promise. God wants to take you out of your grave of flesh and despair.

Out of your carnal thoughts.

Out of your sinful nature.

Out of your self-pity.

Out of your fear of life.

Out of your fear of man.

Out of your fear of self.

Out of your fear of death.

God is waiting to give you a peace that surpasses all understanding. God wants you to know Him when He opens your grave. And when you come out, you will be like that wheat that bends with the storms and winds of life but does not break. Your root will be deep in the word of God and not in the lies of Satan. You will begin to produce seed for the kingdom of God as instructed in *Genesis 1:28* and not for the kingdom of darkness. Your seed will not be strange to God, for the life you live this day forward will be a testimony to the physical as well as the spiritual children you produce in these last days for the kingdom of God.

You can't claim to have God's Spirit today, and when the storms of life hit, you bend and break. *Your whole life is to take dominion over every situation that you confront.* As Christ was baptized in the river Jordan, you are to be baptized in the river of Jesus's blood. You must wash daily in the blood of Christ, *and when you do this,* you will see new mercies morning by morning. God is faithful to us, and we should be faithful to Him. Let me put it this way.

If you cannot be faithful in your relationships,

If you cannot be faithful on your job,

If you cannot be faithful to those you claim to be your friends,

If you cannot be faithful in your church,

If you cannot be faithful in your marriage,

—and all of these are physical relationships—how do you expect to have a spiritually faithful relationship with God?

God says that He will bring us up out of our graves. *Your flesh is your grave. Come out!* You cannot obtain your spiritual inheritance until you come up out of your flesh. You cannot and do not possess the power to bring yourself up out of your *grave*, your flesh. Only Jesus can. So today, as I pray for you, please give your heart to Jesus, for you don't have much time. Just put all of your trust in *Him*; He will renew the garden of your mind, and there will be a change in your heart and a change in your life. I decree this in Jesus's name. Now claim it for yourself and for your family. It is your time to have a change of heart.

CHAPTER 8
Your Wilderness Test

§

"For Pharaoh will say of the children of Israel, They are entangled in the land, the wilderness hath shut them in" (Exod. 14:3).

THIS STORY SHOULD BE FAMILIAR to us all. The scene here is of Moses bringing God's people (the Israelites) out of bondage, out of slavery (out of Egypt), and while leading them to the Promised Land, they had to go through an *entangled wilderness*. These Israelites found themselves between the army of Pharaoh and the Red Sea—between a rock and a hard place. Pharaoh, in a very short period of time, had forgotten the destruction Israel's God had rained down on his empire. And as Pharaoh pursued Israel, he found them boxed in between him and the Red Sea. Israel was ready for the slaughter. Pharaoh was totally unaware that it was he and his army that were about to be destroyed.

So often God uses our enemy, our shortcomings, our fears, and our addictions to aid in the witness of Him working to free us from our enslavement by Satan. Many of us have heard it said, *"Be careful what you pray for."* Anyone who has spent any serious time seeking God and wanting to make godly changes in his or her life can attest to this statement. God will always use your own life to reveal your shortcomings; all of your shortcomings directly identify your resistance to put your *total trust* in God. But this isn't the point I want to make. I want us to focus in on the place where the Israelites were found by Pharaoh soon after they had left Egypt.

Israel moved to Egypt to recover from a famine in their land. When the famine was over, they stayed in Egypt and became slaves. *Please get this.* When you stay too long in a place that God has not promised you, you will become a slave to it. You will become addicted to its lifestyle. You cannot allow the familiarity of that event in your life to keep you looking back when God prepares your exodus. You cannot fear your tomorrow and long for your sinful yesterday. To get to the place God has promised you, you *must* lay to rest your past and take an active part in birthing forth your future.

We will look at Israel's wilderness experience with the hope to help you see the need for your wilderness experience and what should be learned from it. Like Pharaoh, Satan does not want you to leave his territory, your sinful past. He needs you in his camp working his programs. He has gotten so good with his tactics that, like Pharaoh, he will let you escape from his camp only to give you the illusion that the work of God in your life is more painful than what he offers. Our addictions to our sin nature will always cause a carnal withdrawal within us when we attempt to free ourselves from their grip on our emotions and on our way of thinking. You cannot believe everything you think. Those in Narcotics Anonymous (NA) are a mixture of every conceivable addiction there is. Their addiction didn't start with the drug they used. Their addiction started in their mind. In their pursuit to overcome their addiction, they have bonded together, and many of those who have beaten the period of withdrawal have stepped out of their addiction and have found a new family of *recovering* addicts to socialize with.

When new recovering addicts come to the nonprofit organization, they pick a sponsor. The sponsor has been clean of his or her addiction for a long period of time. That sponsor's job is to coach and instruct the newcomer in a manner that will help the newcomer stay clean of the addiction and not return to its use. The problem with the statement "recovering addict" is it provides no finality to the addict's future. The addict will always live in the mental state of thinking that they are "recovering" and never see themselves as "recovered." An unconscious fear of returning to the old behavior is ever present.

In the church, yes, we are saved; yes, we are born again; but we are *recovering sinners*. We can fall back at any time when we think we don't need the counsel of God though the Holy Spirit every day. Each member in the NA has a sponsor, but in the church, not everyone has a spiritual mentor that he or she can talk to when he or she feels the itch to return to sinful habits. Yes they have the Holy Spirit to comfort them, but each born again believer is on assignment to minister the God news of the Gospel to the addicted. When the sinfully addicted person feels that life is too hard, when he or she wants to return to his or her wilderness, this is your opportunity to minister.

What is a wilderness?

a. A tract or region uncultivated and uninhabited by human beings.
b. An area essentially undisturbed by human activity together with its naturally developed life community.
c. An empty or pathless area or region[1]

If I, if you, if we are to be honest with ourselves, there are areas in our lives that are uncultivated and uninhabited by God. We stay away from these areas because they are painful. They are areas that we are uncomfortable with. They are areas that if we visit there, we will find ourselves alone in a mental box where, without God, Satan can begin to play and plant thoughts of death in the garden of our mind. These are the areas of our mind that we don't give total access to God. They are areas where Satan plants his best weeds. Like Israel, we remember our past. We remember our sufferings and we remember our pain, but because we have a fear of the unknown, a fear of our future, a fear of the potentials of a new beginning, we retreat back into our past wilderness experiences. We withdraw back into our sinful nature—a territory uninhabited by God–a sinful area that we are very familiar with.

If the truth be told, it is much easier to stay where we are—in the natural—because we are familiar with those surroundings; we are familiar with the darkness. It is easy to stay there because that suffering and pain have really become the only comfort we know. We have grown accustomed to their effect on our thinking, and to some degree, we crave it. Not only that, but we tend to pass this behavior on to our children. We see others being spiritually prosperous, we see others obtaining the peace of God, but we are too afraid to pass through our wilderness experiences to receive the deliverance of God. The nature of sin in our lives causes us to have many negative experiences as we move through time and live in our flesh. But we should not look at our wilderness experiences as hopeless events. We should look at them as opportunities to define who we are in God.

We are going to have wilderness experiences because God is working in our lives to get us focused on Him so that our deliverance can come and that it can be complete.

When we come into our wilderness, God is telling us to repent.

When we come into our wilderness experiences, God is sending a revival for our soul. The Holy Spirit becomes our comforter, and He is there to help us through our withdrawal from the nature of sin. Not only does He comfort us, but when we get serious about having a relationship with God, the Holy Spirit coaches us in what we should not do and in what we should do to please God. Our willingness to submit to His guidance, instruction and teaching aids in making our withdrawal complete. We are no longer a recovering sinners; we are the recovered sinners whose lives are lived and directed by the Holy Spirit.

Like Israel, when we focus on the natural experiences of our situations, we can become distorted and fearful. But wilderness experiences are designed to show us two distinctive things about ourselves:

1. What we are.
2. What we are not.

The nation of Israel did not wake up one morning to find themselves in slavery. It was a process of four hundred years that brought them to that reality. The name *Egypt* means *"that troubles, oppresses, anguishes."* And like Israel at the time of Joseph, some of us are unaware that we are in a spiritual famine; our homes, our families, our jobs, even our church are not feeding us enough to sustain us spiritually. So instead of feeding on the Word of God ourselves, we feed on the world, and later we find ourselves willfully feeding on unclean spiritual foods. We find ourselves *troubled*, we find ourselves *oppressed*, and we find ourselves in *anguish*.

You know what I'm talking about. There is something you have a taste for; you're hungry, but you just don't know exactly what you're hungry for.

You have been feeding your entire life from the table of time. Now God wants to feed you from His table of eternity.

Israel willfully became the inhabitants of Egypt, the inhabitants of trouble, the inhabitants of oppression, and the inhabitants of anguish. So many today have willfully become the inhabitants of this world with all of its bells and whistles that keep them coming back. Even though it is painful, they have found comfort in that pain because it is all they know, and with many of them, *it is all they want to know.*

Your Drug of Choice

The pains of this life have become the drug of choice for many people. Satan has learned how to cultivate that pain, and we unwisely and unconsciously crave more and more of that pain. Some have become paralyzed to their pain, and this makes it easy for them to inflict pain on others.

My mother told me and my siblings' years ago that "birds of a feather flock together." She was telling us that what and who we hang around, what we flock to, is what we become.

Who do you flock to on your job?

Who do you flock to in your home?

Who do you flock to in your family?

And who do you flock to in your church in an effort to comfort your pain?

Is it your past, the dark yesterday areas of your life, or is it Jesus Christ?

Cultivation is always taking place in each of our minds. The Spirit of God works to till the soil of our mind by digging, by stirring, and by overturning it.

We resist because we think we must be hard, and in being hard, we think this shows our strength, but this is not true. It is very difficult to plant seeds in hard ground. We should become weak as Christ becomes strong in us. Too many confessing Christians want to be strong in their spirit, and they want to be strong in their flesh too. They unknowingly want to keep their flesh active in the affairs of their life. They think their flesh is what gives them life. They think their flesh gives them strength. They forget that their flesh is a shell of who they are and they need to discard that shell in order to become all that God has predestined them to become. To accomplish this, they must be willing to surrender all of their fleshly desires, their wants, and their ambitions for this life to the perfect will of God. He knows far better than any of us the direction our life should take, and He knows how to lead us into that path.

God wants us soft and pliable like wet clay. When we surrender our lives completely to Him, He will mold us day by day into creatures prepared for a glorious eternity with Him.

The more time we spend in His word and in His hand, the more His word digs into our inner man to reveal and deliver us from our sin nature—our spots, our wrinkles, and our blemishes.

The more time we spend in His word, the more His word stirs up the stench of our sins, enabling us to see how filthy we really are and how much we need the blood of Christ to cleanse us.

The more time we spend in His word, the more His word overturns our worldly minded agenda and gives us new direction.

If we are not careful, the destructive nature of a carnal life will make us hard-hearted and not fit for the kingdom of God.

The work of Satan in people's lives can freezer-burn their outer and inner core and make it so destructively hard that the love of God and the love for mankind will be alien to their nature and to their character.

Aliens

An alien is a foreigner, especially one who is not a naturalized citizen of the country where he or she is living. Born-again believers should accept the fact that they are aliens here on this earth and not claim citizenship here. We live here, but we do not belong here. We are passing through. There is a better place prepared for us. Our purpose here, however, is to lead lost souls out of this pit of darkness and into a lifesaving relationship with Jesus. But if we continue to spend time absorbing the nature of this cursed earth, we will continue to be cursed. However, when we realize that this cursed earth (our flesh) is not our home, like Israel with Moses, we will have to spend some time in the wilderness and make a final decision to sacrifice our flesh for the maturing of our soul and spirit. We must choose to be transformed into what God created us for or return back to our flesh (Egypt) and stay in bondage to the ways of the world.

I stated earlier that part of the definition for wilderness is *uninhabited, undisturbed by human activity*. This explains why each of us needs the wilderness. We have been so bombarded with human things, human issues, human ideas, human thought, and human systems that the purity of the gospel has been misplaced in our thinking. Just as the industrial world has slowly polluted this planet, the works of Satan has slowly polluted our minds.

We want to humanize the Word of God so it will fit into the box we make for it. Human thought is not in the mind of God. Human thought is centered on itself and its sinful nature. There are some confessing Christians who respond to, act like, live like, and talk like what they determine is *the way*. They have not allowed the Spirit of God to circumcise their flesh but have willingly spiritually castrated themselves and others.

This spiritual castration has hindered the church greatly from reproducing godly children for God's kingdom.

Like the Pharisees and Sadducees, they add and take from the law and attempt to force God's children to adhere to them, not to God. It isn't holy unless they make it so. So instead of building God's kingdom, they become the demolition team, and like Pharaoh, they put others into slavery causing them to never come to know their full spiritual potential because they measure their lives by the standard set forth by the Pharisees, the Sadducees, and their Pharaoh and not the standard of God. *Shame on us!*

CROSS YOUR RED SEA AT ANY COST

God's people were fearful and felt defeated when *they* came to the conclusion that they were trapped between Pharaoh's army and the Red Sea. They were suffering from spiritual amnesia. Their fear of the unknown, because they were not used to the move of God in their lives, allowed their present circumstances to paralyze their future. But God always has a plan for His children. Even though they were strange children, God desired to raise them up to their full spiritual potential.

Jesus's desire is to fulfill and have us fulfill all righteousness. He is the light of the world, the light in the garden of your mind. He has experienced your wilderness. He has passed through the wilderness of time and has become the example to show us how to get through this wilderness and gloriously enter into the Promised Land of the eternity He has prepared for us.

Matthew 4:1 reads: "Then was Jesus led up by the Spirit into the wilderness to be tempted (tested) by Satan (the devil)."

Jesus's time in the wilderness was no different than anyone else's. He was tempted to feed the earthly hungers of His flesh, which would have killed His hunger for God. Please note that in the natural, we hunger (lust) for many things in the flesh, but when we repent and turn from our wicked ways and make a decision to take a slow walk through our wilderness in our mind garden with God by our side, like Jesus, we begin to hunger (lust) only for the food of God—His word.

As Jesus realized that He was an alien to this world, He embraced it so that He could show us how to overcome it. We too have to embrace this world in order to aid in the transition of those souls seeking Christ. *Winning lost souls to Christ should rank at the top of our life agenda.* Jesus was tempted by lust. Many of us have limited lust to a sexual concept, but in reality carnal lust is an emotional feeling of intense desire for anything other than God. Anytime we do things to bring attention to ourselves, not God, be assured, we are operating in the spirit of lust.

Jesus was also tempted by worldly desires. Church, Satan wants to give you the treasures of this world. God wants to give you all of His kingdom treasure. You cannot possess both. You can have wealth, but be careful. So many today don't just want to have wealth. They want to possess it. If you possess earthly wealth and your intentions for that wealth are not the intentions of God, you will become earthly possessive and spiritually bankrupt. But when you possess spiritual wealth, you will become spiritually possessive and begin feeding on the world—the spiritual treasures of the kingdom of God. You will emulate the nature of Christ in the places you go, in the things you do, and in the words you speak. *Proverbs 30:7–9* reads: "Two things have I required of thee; deny them not to me before I die. Remove far from me vanity and lies; give me neither poverty nor riches; feed me with food convenient for me. Lest I be full and deny thee, and say, who is the Lord? Or lest I be poor and steal, and take the name of my God in vain."

So, are you earthly/worldly possessive, or are you spiritually/kingdom of God possessive? You cannot possess both at the same time. Jesus tells us in *Matthew 6:24*: "No man can serve two masters; for either he will hate the one, and love the other; or else he will hold to the one, and despise the other. Ye cannot serve God and mammon (money)."

There is someone today entering into your wilderness experience.

There is someone today who is in the center of your wilderness experience.

And there is someone else today who is coming out of your wilderness experience.

I suggest that wherever you find yourself today (right now), *don't look back*. Revival is at the threshold of your mind garden. God is planting good seed deep into your mind's soil so that you will produce good fruit. You don't have to be anxious for your life because you know God will supply all that you need for this life according to His riches in glory. This is exactly where Eve and Adam missed their blessing. Through the lies of Satan, they thought they needed more. Remember, God had already supplied everything they needed. So what they thought was a need was really a want.

Like children, many of us are still functioning as carnal children in our mind garden and in church and have not matured into spiritual adulthood. We have no effective, consistent witness for God's kingdom. *We like visiting, but we don't want to move in*. We don't want our true selves revealed so we move from church to church, never facing and defeating our demons.

The reason we don't want to move in is the same principle that applies to the natural. In my natural father's house, there are conditions that I must abide by in order for me to say there. In my home, there are conditions for my adult children to abide by. Failure to comply will result in eviction. But if I truly love my father and my children truly love me, I will know my father's heart, and my children will know my heart. I'll know that the conditions for my residency with my father are out of my submission to the requirements placed on me as his child. The same with my children. Even though they are adults, they will always have the responsibility to respect and honor how I run my house. God is a God of order. He corrects and removes chaos from His presence. We too have the direct responsibility to remove all chaos from our lives. This will not happen while we operate with carnal characteristics. This will happen, however, when we operate in the character of Christ. When we submit to the requirements of our heavenly father, we are always welcomed into His Kingdom.

Today is the day for all of us to make up our minds, discard some old stuff and pack up some new stuff, and move in with God—to come home.

Yes! Just for a little while longer, we will have wilderness experience because we are going through carnal withdrawal, but God is well able to keep us and deliver us from our addiction to sin. Like Jesus, are you led by God's Spirit, or is there someone else in the natural that you are allowing to lead you?

Are you surrendering to Christ? Are you taking His hand and walking with Him? Today is an excellent day to say good-bye to your wilderness. Today you are putting your total trust in God and your Savior, Jesus Christ. Remember, your mind is a wilderness. It picks up some of everything that your life experiences blow through it. In short, our mind is like tumbleweed. We have given the winds of life free rein to blow us in any direction they want. *Do not believe everything your mind thinks.*

Extraterrestrials

Numerous movies have set a plot that centers on aliens, extraterrestrials, visiting earth for one of two reasons. One, they were lost and just wanted to go home (*ET*). Or two, they want to take the earth and eradicate the human race from it (*War of the Worlds* and *The Day the Earth Stood Still*). The latter is what is happening now. Satan and all the demonic forces that he controls are residents of this earth (*Luke 4:1–6*). He is the prince of the power of the air, and we are in his territory for one purpose: *to win*. We are in a spiritual war. Satan is not taking any prisoners. He wants to keep all of us dead in our sins, focused on death, not on our life in Christ. He does not want any one of us to be born again and resurrected. He wants us to live like him—forever separated from God and forever chained under darkness. His choice was to stay in his wilderness, narcissist. You have the choice right now to either live eternally with Satan or eternally with God. Please choose wisely so that you can pass your wilderness tests. None of us can live too long with just ourselves. This is why God said that it was not God for man to be alone. You are never alone when you have Christ in your life.

CHAPTER 9
Draw Me, Lord

§

All that the Father giveth me shall come to me; and him that cometh to me I will in no wise cast out.

For I came down from heaven not to do mine own will but the will of Him that sent me.

And this is the Father's will who hath sent me, that of all that He hath given me I should lose nothing, but should raise it up again at the last day.

And this is the will of Him that sent me that everyone who seeth the Son, and believeth on Him, may have everlasting life; and I will raise him up on the last day.

The Jews then murmured at Him, because he said, I am the bread that came down from heaven.

And they said, is not this Jesus, the son of Joseph, whose father and mother we know? How is it then that he saith, I came down from heaven?

Jesus, therefore answered and said unto them, Murmur not among yourselves.

No man can come to me, except the Father, who hath sent me, draw him; and I will raise him up on the last day (*John 6:37–44*).

IN THIS SCRIPTURE TEXT, JESUS is revealing Himself to this Jewish community and tells them that He is the bread of life sent from God. Earlier in this chapter, Jesus fed more than five thousand men, not including the women and children, who came to hear Him speak. The miracle was His feeding this multitude with only five barley loaves and two small fish. After the multitude had dinned scrumptiously, Jesus's disciples gathered and filled twelve baskets with the leftovers of the food—one for each disciple. Can you imagine the time it took them to collect the scraps?

In an effort to avoid being taken by force and heralded *king of the Jews* by the people who witnessed this miracle, Jesus separated Himself from his disciples and the crowd and went into the mountain region alone. I believe He went to spend some quite time with His Father. After His communion with his Father and under the cover of night, Jesus pursued his disciples not by boat but by walking on water. When the crowd realized that He (Jesus) was no longer in their territory, they got into boats and sailed across the sea to find Him.

Let me put a pin here and make a point. The majority of these people were fixed on the miracles that Jesus performed—outward blessings. They had no interest in receiving kingdom seed from God into the garden of their mind—inner blessing. They were not interested in fellowshipping with Jesus; they wanted more signs and more wonders.

There are Christians today who are hunting, searching, seeking, and looking for this apostle, that prophet, this evangelist, that pastor, that spiritual teacher, all in an attempt to receive a word from God, to get an external blessing, to witness a miracle from God, but they are not seeking any intimate time with Him—prayer. They are lukewarm, and like those whom they follow, they focus on getting something for themselves, never willing to give their life for the cause of Christ. They are not paying any attention to those who practice charismatic witchcraft—those wolves who have crept into the church with an inversion of spiritual works (i.e., those persons using prayer, prophetic gifts, and words of wisdom to manipulate others and attempt to manipulate God for self-serving purposes). They pursue physical signs and wonders and not the spiritual things of God. They can't see that they have become like the ones they despise because of their own blindness. They chase after material rewards and discard spiritual blessings.

They have been going to Christian assemblies of their choosing for years upon years, mastering the protocol of that assembly and others. They have just enough Word of God in them to seem godly, but they have no relationship with their Lord and Savior. They have yet to deeply study the Bible (the Word of God) for themselves to show themselves approved by God and to make the necessary changes in their lives to be called His son. They are so busy searching for physical evidence of an anointing and searching for human recognition that they are missing out on becoming the anointed of God and on becoming a life-giving blessing to His body—you and me.

They express their opinion on a given subject with no authority. They may not make a loud announcement of their opinion, but be assured, their quiet and soft verbal comments are another way to stir a negative reaction from the listener for the truth they are murmuring about.

We need to remember God created us in His image and in His likeness (*Genesis 1:26*). Satan wants us to leave our creator and serve him (*Genesis 3:1–6*). He wants us to believe a death-producing lie, and a lie is just what the flesh craves. The truth about the flesh is that it wants what it wants when it wants it. Its only concept of fulfillment is to be satisfied *now* regardless of the negative consequences those actions will have on its soul. This is exactly what happened to Esau, Jacob's brother. He wanted food now and sold his birthright to get fed in the natural. Don't give up your eternal rights to be satisfied with the carnal things of this world.

> And Jacob boiled pottage: and Esau came from the field, and he was faint:
>
> And Esau said to Jacob, Feed me, with that same red pottage; for I am faint: therefore was his name called Edom.
>
> And Jacob said, Sell me this day thy birthright.
>
> And Esau said, Behold, I am at the point to die: and what profit shall this birthright do to me?

And Jacob said, Swear to me this day; and he swear unto him: and he sold his birthright unto Jacob.

Then Jacob gave Esau bread and pottage of lentils; and he did eat and drink, and rose up, and went his way: thus Esau despised his birthright (*Gen. 25:29–34*).

THE ADAM IN YOU

Like Esau, we have two major problems that will keep us from being able to claim our godly birthright:

(1) We demand from others their service to please our own fleshly hungers.
(2) When we feel faint and weak, we will sell our soul (kingdom birthright) in order to satisfy a carnal, worldly, fleshly desire.

Like the boiling soup, Esau's pride, his arrogance, and his aggressive attitude were his downfall. When anything is hot, you do best to handle it wisely, and this is what Jacob did. Now this red soup that Jacob prepared can be applied metaphorically like the word *adom*, which is close to the name Edom. Edom almost sounds like Adam – red clay. Jacob made the soup from earthly items which made the soup look red. God made man from red clay. So, as you can see, Esau's actions are like his great grandfather Adam's. He gave up his birthright in order to satisfy an earthly lust. Sin has caused the flesh, the carnal man, Adam to rebel against God just like Satan did. Because of this Adam, man has made it his lifework to become like God. Esau gave up his birth right for food. Adam – man – gave up his birth right for disobedience. Both put their flesh before their destiny. The days of the Tower of Babel are upon us. We are claiming our greatness on our own merit, not on the mercies of God. Like Belteshazzar (Daniel), Hananiah (Sharach), Mishael (Meshach), and Azariah (Abednego), if the church doesn't go along with the world's agenda, the church is subject to be cast into the fiery furnace or into the lion's den. We need to get our priorities straight. The church is choosing the world and not God.

The System

Can you remember the last time you examined, inspected, checked, or tested a statement to see if it had any truth, or did you just believe and receive it because someone you trusted in the flesh or who seemed deep and spiritual to you told it to you? What have you believed that drew you in the direction that you have now taken for your life? What have you believed that drew you to feel what you feel, think like you think, and act like you act?

We need to repent of the behavioral seed of personal destruction planted by this world system, which causes us to drink in deeply of the chaos of this life. Like a live frog being boiled in a pot of water, we have become so comfortable – so numb – with this world's system, we unconsciously sit patiently until we are done. The warmth of a carnal life causes one to find comfort in it and in it alone. It camouflages our reality and causes one to seek the comfort of its warmth and of its darkness. The will of God is to draw us out of this darkness, out of this heat and into His loving arms, into the warm light of eternal life and fellowship with Him.

Jesus' will is to do the Father's will. Look at *John 6:39* again. "And this is the Father's will who sent me, that of all that He hath given me I should lose nothing, but should raise it up again at the last day." Each of us must give our will to Jesus. We must come to Him and submit to His perfect will in our lives in order to truly live. Think about it. He wants to raise us up again. Did you catch that? Raise us up again. Just like a prince who was born in and raised in poverty, we find ourselves in the same condition. Not only have we become use to our improvised condition spiritually, but we can't seem to get our mind around the fact that if we truly have accepted Christ into our lives, we are now joint heirs to a royal bloodline. We are so earthly minded in these last days that we squander our spiritual wealth pursuing earthly treasures because we are addicted to an emotional drug called recognition from others.

Can anyone explain why in such a time like this so many of our family members, our friends, and our neighbors are lost? Could it be that they have not yet been drawn to Christ? It makes sense to me. What are you doing about it? *John 17:21–23* reads: "That they all may be one, as thou, Father, are in me, and I in thee, that they also may be one in us; that the world may believe that thou hast sent me. And the glory which thou gavest me I have given them that they may be one, even as we are one; I in them, and thou in me, that they may be made perfect in me; and that the world may know that thou hast sent me, and hast loved them as thou hast loved me."

Since the time of Abel and Cain, this earth has longed for revenge. Whatever this world can do against you, it will do it. It has all but alienated and eliminated a Christian's zeal to witness to his or her family, friends, and neighbors. It goes without saying that if we are not witnessing to these individuals, what chance does the person, the cult, the nation that doesn't like you have to hear the gospel preached to them by you? The world wants you to keep your witness inside the walls of the church building; inside of yourself, and many today have complied with that request. The ministering of the gospel to a dying world in today's social environment is unacceptable by its world governments. Because so many people don't want to hear the truth about their ungodly selected lifestyle outside of organized religion, they say *"preach to yourselves, not us." Like Christ*, when we shine light onto their darkness, we must be ready to be crucified and should *find rest in the crucifying of our flesh, for this frees us from all fear of the world*. When you come into the understanding of the condition of this world, you will begin to see the need for Christ in your life. You will live to be more like Christ, you will live for Christ, and this will be your power to overcome the world like He did.

To be one in Christ, we must first do what Jesus preached. *Matthew 4:17* reads: "From that time Jesus began to preach, and say, 'Repent; for the kingdom of heaven is at hand.'" Before the garden of our mind can receive the holy seed of God, each of us must first repent. We must turn away from our sinful nature and turn to Christ. We must begin to think godly, walk godly, and live godly. We must reconsider our present line of thought and shift it from earthly to heavenly, from Gentile to Saint, from fleshly to holy. Let the revival begin in your mind so that there may be a revival in your soul. Revive us O Lord!

Immediately after we make that connection with Christ, we have been commanded to *go*. We must be ready to die to our flesh and be raised in the spirit. We must crucify our flesh. We can't wait on the apostle, the evangelist, the prophet, the pastor, or the teacher to witness to the lost. Each of us now has been commanded to be a witness to the world. *Matthew 28:20* reads: "Go ye, therefore, and teach all nations, baptizing them in the name of the Father, and of the Son, and of the Holy Ghost." Just take what you know of Christ and speak it into the lives of those you come into contact with. God will give you what you need to share with them. Please understand that as you eat of His word and digest it, it will give you the necessary spiritual nutrients to strengthen your spirit man causing you to regurgitate His words in your everyday conversation. You will find yourself speaking only what He speaks to you. In other words, your conversation will change.

Since the spiritual fall of Adam and Eve, this world has been baptized into the lust of the flesh, the lust of the eye, and the pride of life. God wants to raise us up out of that baptism and baptize us into Himself, into His Son, and into the Holy Spirit. This will not and cannot take place unless we are drawn to Him and baptized in the blood of Christ. And because so many resist the drawing power of Christ in their lives by not acknowledging His Lordship over their lives, *they have allowed the law of the land to supersede the promises of God.* They have been given up to a reprobate mind. Whatever they can imagine is OK to them.

North America spent over ninety million dollars over a Valentine Day weekend to see a movie that glorified the lust of the flesh; it was a vivid illustration of the moral fiber of the nation sinking deeper and deeper into a cesspool of fornication, lust, and idolatry. And this is called entertainment.

We say now, *"Entertain me. I don't need saving; I need entertainment."* We feel that there is no need to repent, to give up the fellowship of this world for fellowship with Christ. According to the standards of this world system, I'm OK. This world's seed—its media—has bombarded our mind garden with so much violence, so much sex, so much lust, so much hate, and so much dependency on it. This mind-set has caused many people today to not know or even attempt to conceptualize what is right and what is wrong. To them the concept of right and wrong is centered in what they feel at the moment, what they think at the moment, what they want in the moment, and what they have been taught by media. They have no need for the Word of God and the perfect will of God in their lives.

The church! Many of us have missed it. We have become like our children. We want to stay inside the church house and play church games. We have become sluggish with the spiritual board game of spiritual complacency. We have become obese with a lust for this world with no spiritual action or exercise. We are unaware of the danger we are in by not fighting the good fight of faith, and we have lost the will to fight. We openly and verbally challenge one another's spiritual maturity but don't want to challenge those on our block, in our neighborhoods, in our communities, and in our government. The reason for this is because our own lives are not measuring up to what we are confessing, and the world knows it. We are not conquering; we are retreating.

We fight and belittle one another with the assumption that from our life's experiences, we are qualified to teach our brothers and sisters in God's house valuable lessons on God's kingdom. We don't encourage those who stumble. We don't spend time trying to know one another—not in a negative way, but in ways that not only build them up but build us up as well. We can really take some pointers from the NA. We have no people skills. If anyone is looking for the real scandal, just tune in to the "My Church Network," your assembled body of believers, and watch. Each episode is guaranteed to leave you with your mouth hanging wide open.

Now, before you judge what I just stated, take time to read *Matthew 25:34–40*.

Then shall the King say unto them on his right hand, Come, ye blessed of my father, inherit the kingdom prepared for you from the foundation of the world.

For I was hungry and ye gave me food; I was thirsty and ye gave me drink; I was a stranger and ye took me in;

Naked, and ye clothed me; I was sick and ye visited me; I was in prison, and ye came unto me.

Then shall the righteous answer Him saying, Lord when saw we thee hungry and fed thee; or thirsty and gave thee drink?

When saw we thee a stranger, and took thee in; or naked and clothed thee?

Or when saw we thee sick or in prison and came unto thee?

And the King shall answer and say unto them. Verily I say unto you. In as much as ye have done it unto one of the least of these my brethren, ye have done it unto me.

My brothers and sisters, we are commanded to go into the world and come to Him. If you have come to Him, if you today have claimed that God has drawn you to Him though the power of His word and His Spirit, then you need to get excited about going into the battle ground of this world to make disciples of everyone you meet. How do you do this? You do it:

- By feeding them the bread of life, which will strengthen them for the spiritual battles ahead.
- By giving them a deep drink of God's Spirit, which will wash them on the inside.
- By befriending them and showing yourself faithful to their spiritual maturity.
- By forgiving their sins and shortcomings and casting them into the sea of forgiveness.

- By applying the Word of God like an ointment to their spiritual wounds and sicknesses.
- And by destroying the lies of Satan, who tells them that they are lost and have no hope.

In love, witness to the crimes they have committed against the gospel, remembering that you stand at the threshold of the same type of behavior. Your leading them to a heart of repentance will win them for the Kingdom of God.

We have a lot of work to do for the kingdom of our God. We first must be willing to preach and teach ourselves in the word of God. God will do the rest. Our lives should be a sermon read by men everyday. Let us commit ourselves today to the work of this gospel, this good news. Let us not allow any perceived priority to take priority over our calling. We are favored by God to complete the earthly assignment given to us. Don't bury your gift. Nurture it and see what God does with it. Let Him draw you into the light of your salvation.

CHAPTER 10
A Need to Read

§

EVERYONE AND EVERYTHING ON THIS planet has a need. We need air, we need water, we need rain, we need the rays from the sun, we need shelter, we need clothing, and we need food, to name a few. Outside of the necessities of life, however, everything else becomes a want. "I want this, you want that, and we want something else." It is fascinating to me how we have more wants than needs. If you were to take inventory of all the things in your home, you will find that you have mostly items that you wanted and few that are actually needed. Because of this, not too many people are comprehending the big picture. We place our demands—our wants—on others predicated on what we want from them, not on what we can give them. Some have developed the disease of hoarding, which causes them to seek out things from other people and suffer economically to obtain more stuff.

In this twenty-first century, there is another need that has gone neglected and is causing many to suffer unnecessarily. Yes, you guessed it; it is the *need to read*. Luke 6:2-5 tells us:

> "And certain of the Pharisees said unto them, why do ye that which is not lawful to do on the Sabbath days?
> And Jesus answering them, said, Have ye not read as much as this, what David did, when he was hunger, and they who were with him;

How he went into the house of God and did take and eat the showbread, and gave also to them that were with him; which it is not lawful to eat, but for the priests alone?

And he said unto them, the Son of man is Lord also of the Sabbath."

The definition for *read* is:
Transitive Verb:

1 a (1): To receive or take in the sense of (as letters or symbols) especially by sight or touch. (2): To study the movements of (as lips) with mental formulation of the communication expressed. (3): To utter aloud the printed or written words of <*read* them a story>

3a: To learn the nature of by observing outward expression or signs (read him like a book).

3b: To note the action or characteristics of in order to anticipate what will happen <a good canoeist *reads* the rapids> <a golfer *reading* a green>; *also*: to predict the movement of (a putt) by reading a green.

3c: To anticipate by observation of an opponent's position or movement.[1]

Reading opens the door for knowledge and wisdom. God is pure knowledge and pure wisdom. His word (the Bible) has been given to us because He wants to fellowship with us and redeem us from our sin nature. As we read His word, we open up opportunities to know Him like never before. We literally become like Him. As an auto mechanic has to read the auto manual in order to identify and correct a maintenance problem with a vehicle, the Christian is presented with the Word of God in order to identify and correct his spiritual problem. By uprooting the weeds of Satan out of his mind garden as he moves into the light of God's goodness and mercy towards him, the Christian now becomes a disciple of Christ and lives a life that causes others to want to be saved from their sins as well.

I want to briefly examine the two primary approaches to reading as shown in the definitions presented above. One deals specifically with what is written, and the other deals specifically with what one can see, anticipate, or discern about a person or a situation.

Those of us who read tend to limit our reading to subjects that we like or to emotional territories that don't force our set way of thinking to be tampered with. In short, we read mainly books, magazines, blogs, and so on that we like. We ignore or discard those we don't like or those that don't agree with our philosophy. When people do this, they miss the challenge of strengthening and maturing their faith. Let me say it like this: God is always moving. The problem in the earth realm is we too often tend to sit back and neglect the fact that His whole design is for us to be moving just like Him. *Genesis 2:15* states: "And the Lord God took the man and put him into the Garden of Eden to dress it and to keep it." *Matthew 28:19* states: "Go ye therefore, and teach all nations, baptizing them in the name of the Father and of the Son, and of the Holy Ghost." *Acts 1:8* reads: "But ye shall receive power, after that the Holy Ghost is come upon you: and ye shall be witnesses unto me both in Jerusalem, and in all Judaea, and in Samaria, and unto the uttermost part of the earth." The opportunity exists in the world today for the born-again Christian to reach the uttermost parts of the earth, and they don't all have to go abroad to do it. It can happen right in or near their own neighborhood. There are approximately 254 countries in the world, and there are about 198 nationalities living in North America.

Each of us, until we are called to go home to be with the Lord, are mandated to plant spiritual seed in the minds of all with whom we come into contact. It shouldn't matter to you if they want to hear it or not. The important thing is for you to, in love, plant seeds of repentance in the lives of all in whom you meet daily. After someone plants the spiritual seed, someone else waters that spiritual seed, and God nurtures it until it takes root and germinates in the heart of a person's soul. This will then prepare that soul for the harvest of God. Please don't think that this job belongs to someone other than you. If you are born again, God has equipped you through the Holy Spirit to meet the needs of His people. He has sent you into this world as an ambassador for His kingdom. You are a spiritually accredited diplomat sent by God as His official representative on this earth. To complete your assignment, you must become an authority on what He wants, what He offers, and what is needed in the life of the individual that you are leading to Christ. You must be committed to following Christ and not be self-serving even when your faith is shaken. Not one of us can allow our focus to be broken. It's either Him or self. If you are in Him, there is no self to satisfy. Everything you do is out of your love for God, your love for your neighbor, and your desire to please God.

BROKEN FOCUS

Broken focus is why marriages fail. One or both partners stop focusing on and putting their mate first. They begin to focus on their carnal, worldly wants, not on the spiritual need of their mate. Their focus is now broken. When this happens, they fail to follow the truth and begin to neglect their mate. *"Your ability to die to yourself and to fulfill the needs of someone else is the greatest sacrifice you can offer to God."* Some think, however, that their possessions are the most important thing to either get or give in a marriage. Loving sacrifice is what God is looking for from us as we focus on our purpose on earth and our destiny in the kingdom of God.

Let's return to the garden. *James 1:8* reads: "A double minded man is unstable in all his ways." *Proverbs 3:5–6* reads: "Trust in the lord with all thine heart; and lean not unto thine own understanding. In all thy ways acknowledge him and he shall direct thy paths." You may have heard it said in church circles that *"Anything with two heads is a freak."* The root of this meaning is very true in the spiritual world. Note again that Adam and Eve were not to eat from the tree in the center of the garden, which was named "the tree of the knowledge of good and evil." God knew that man's soul was not ready; it had not matured enough to handle evil. God knew that in man's infant mental state, he was weak and needed time to mature into the spiritual man God had set forth for him to become.

Yes, everything that God created is good, and God's plan has always been to raise up children who will emulate His character and nature. Man's childlike nature was not fully in tune with the plan God had for him. Satan knew this and planted the seed needed for man to sin. I Samuel 22b tells us that: "Behold, to obey is better than sacrifice, and to hearken than the fat of rams."

Just like with Job, Satan counted on man's spiritual weakness to be the calling card for his lies and treachery. Satan, in an attempt to be like God (*Isa. 14:14*), set the stage for his acts of treason against his creator and his acts of terrorism against you and me. God said, *"I AM"*; Satan said, *"I will."* Satan attempted to *will* himself into a position, but he did not have the means to possess it. Whenever our will goes against the plans and purposes that the *"I am"* has set forth, we, like Satan, *sin*. Did you get that? Satan is a sinner too, and all the hosts in heaven that followed him are sinners. Each of us should hunger for the mind of God in our lives; however, the sin nature in us causes us to be double-minded and hunger for the mind of Satan in our flesh and thirst for God in our spirit. Note that verse 6 of Proverbs 3 tells us that God will direct our paths (plural). Each of us is walking a different pathway. There are many pathways that lead to death and destruction, but there is only one path that leads to righteous living and a holy lifestyle. We are in a constant war with our flesh and with our spirit to choose which path to take each and every day of our lives here on this earth. This is why we must read. *2 Timothy 2:15* states: "Study to shew thyself approved unto God, a workman that needeth not to be ashamed, rightly dividing the word of truth." There is only one God. Neither Satan nor you nor I can replace Him or come equal to His glory. Sin has caused us to take many paths to destruction. God's word directs us to the single path that leads us into eternal fellowship with Him as we regain our focus.

Our focus becomes broken when we take our eyes off the prize. God planted something in each of us that He wants to mature. Your spirit must mature and become one with His Spirit. This is the marriage that Satan is so fearful of and attempts so diligently to keep us from realizing. We have not begun to fathom our full kingdom potential. So many have been blinded by Satan with the veil of lust, the veil of deceit, the veil of anger, the veil of hate, and the veil of murder. Too many of our brothers and sisters in Christ are missing the mark of the high calling of God simply because their focus is not on the eternal. Their focus is on the right now. Their focus is on the temporal. *Everything that they envision is time based, not eternity based.* They only see battles and have not looked, studied, and read to see how we, the sons of God, overcome by the blood of the Lamb. God is always working to get us onto the right path.

> And the angel of the Lord spake unto Philip, saying, Arise, and go toward the south unto the way that goeth down from Jerusalem unto Gaza, which is desert.
>
> And he arose and went: and, behold, a man of Ethiopia, a eunuch of great authority under Candace queen of the Ethiopians, who had the charge of all her treasure, and had come to Jerusalem for to worship.
>
> Was returning, and sitting in his chariot read Esaias the prophet.
>
> Then the Spirit said unto Philip, Go near, and join thyself to this chariot.
>
> And Philip ran thither to him and heard him read the prophet Esaias, and said, Understandest thou what thou readest?
>
> And he said, "How can I, except some man should guide me? And he desired Philip that he would come up and sit with him" (*Acts 8:26–31*).

Did you notice that God's initial command to Philip was simple to go? No further instructions were given. Philip responded and while he was on the road he met a man and witnessed to him, Christ. It now becomes the responsibility of each born-again believer in Christ to be an effective witness like Philip. This is accomplished in acts of love and an aggressive will to be led by the Holy Ghost. Satan knows he is defeated, but some of us don't believe it because we still are operating in our flesh. We have broken focus. We claim victory until an earthly catastrophe shifts our vision from spiritual to carnal. We then become little gods and want to assist God in changing the catastrophe into a blessing, not realizing that it already is a blessing. Everything that God does has a purpose. Paul felt that his physical infirmity was a hindrance to his ministry (*2 Cor. 12:9*). Let me say this, and I pray I offend no one: The moment you were born into this earth, you began to live. But you also started the process of decay and death. Answer this question: Why do you want to stay here? If you had any response other than *"to win lost souls to Christ,"* you have chosen the wrong reason, and you have broken focus.

Jesus was our greatest example. Now for those of you who are married and have families, the vision is still the same, and it will never change. As I stated earlier in this chapter, when couples operate in broken focus, self becomes the center of their attention, not Christ. Philip in *Acts 8* was so willing to follow the leading of an angel of God that he not only witnessed to a man in power, but his witness impacted the queen of Ethiopia. This eunuch that Philip shared the good news of Christ with was over the treasures of Ethiopia; he had gone to Jerusalem to worship, and while traveling on his way home from the worship service, he met Philip. It wasn't by coincidence that Philip was passing by. It is not by coincidence that you were born and then born again. It is also not a coincidence that opportunities are presented to you every day, but you fail to act on them. *If all of us would listen to the angel of God, if we would listen to the Holy Spirit, our impact in the earth realm would be the same as Philip's.* This eunuch was reading scripture without an understanding. He needed someone to break it down for him in bite-size pieces.

I had to learn the hard way that you can't feed the whole gospel to children. Now, when I say *children*; that is exactly what I mean. Just like with Adam and Eve, you should not be so quick to classify a person in the church mature predicated on his or her age. This is not always true. Some people are mature in physical age but are novices (childlike) in spiritual things. This was the case with Adam and Eve. They were mature in physical form but infants in spiritual form. They just didn't understand.

We must get an understanding of the things of God in order to follow him – in order to live for Him. In my thirty + years of ministry, I have come across numerous individuals in their thirties, their forties, their fifties, their sixties, and their seventies who have been in church most of their lives almost, and that is all they know. *They know church work, but they don't know the work of the church.* It's like talking a foreign language to them. The majority of their Bible study has taken place only on Sunday morning and in a weekly Bible study, with no spiritual application of the word of God in their lives throughout the week. Like Satan, they know scripture forward and backward, but they have no application skills. *They are not being transformed; they just have been informed.* This has caused a carnal-natured epidemic in the house of God. The love of many has waxed cold. A true, godly love has lost its meaning in our lives, and now every man is for himself.

Mind Bouncer

When I visited nightclubs in my youth, some of them had individuals near the door called bouncers. Their whole purpose was to ensure that no troublemakers got in. If there was going to be a fight, it started at the door and was swiftly moved outside. This ensured that the individuals who had gathered inside were able to enjoy themselves without the threat of physical assault. One of the purposes of the Holy Spirit is that of a spiritual weed bouncer. His role is to guard and guide our minds into a deeper revelation of God's goodness and mercies toward us. He also guides and leads us into all righteousness. This is the reason we must read and apply the word of God to our mind daily. *We have too many men trying to be men and too many women trying to be women*, and none of them are trying to live like the sons and daughters of God that they have been called to be. All natural, no spiritual.

When we live like this, we are quick to reject the Holy Spirit as our mind bouncer. When we operate in the natural, we get natural results. When we operate in the spiritual, we get spiritual results. Some are operating in their own strength. We think we paid for our ticket to get into the kingdom party. No! Christ paid it all for us. We failed to bring our mind bouncer with us and this allows Satan access into our mind to plant weeds of destruction. We believe that with the little anointing that we have, while we are on this spiritual journey, we are equipped for the works of Satan, our adversary. Satan is catching so many of us off guard before we get to the party. Throughout the history of man, Satan has known that our self-centered will causes us to want to lead, not follow. We want to be in charge and not submit. We want the recognition, not the resurrection. So he catches us at the door – at the threshold of our anointing – and sale us fake treasures; dead works.

Note that the eunuch not only went to Jerusalem to worship, but while he was on his way home, he read scripture in an attempt to strengthen his faith. He knew his position in the earth realm, but more importantly, he wanted to know his position in the kingdom of God. *This eunuch had the title, and he had the treasure; now he sought the truth.* We can no longer passively read the Word of God. Our lives depend directly upon our willingness to deny our flesh and to become absorbed in the truth. Each of us must become the truth of God in the lives of those we impact every day. We are fascinated with so many other things and not the Word of God. Let us check ourselves. Let us study to show ourselves worthy. Let us die to ourselves and live in Christ. In order to live for Christ, the Christian most die to his flesh – self. Self is the sin problem for man and in order to overcome sin, we have to deny every carnal and lustful want in our flesh. Die to it. Die to your carnal self. Making your primary need in life be living for Jesus and for Him alone is the greatest decision you can make in life. When you get this need right, you will realize that you have won the spiritual fight. *What else is there to want?*

HERE COMES THE JUDGE

Have you heard this saying: *"Your first impression is the most important"*? Jesus showed us that impressions can be changed. Do you remember the story of Saul before his name was changed to Paul (*Acts 9*)? The first reading on his character showed him causing many Christians to fear for their lives. He persecuted the church and breathed out threats against it. But while he was on his way to carry out what he thought was right, what he thought was truth, what he thought was his duty, he met Jesus. He met him on the Damascus road. Saul traveled an estimated 168.3 miles from Jerusalem to Damascus to persecute what he thought was a cult of men and women called Christians who followed Christ. But his earthly assignment was changed to a spiritual one. With his assignment changed by Jesus, Saul's name was changed. His name was changed to his Roman birth name of Paul because it was more intune with his spiritual assignment to the Gentiles. With Paul's becaming an apostle of Christ, he too now was persecuted. Like the nature of Saul, this world is quick to judge in accordance with its carnal thinking or its religious philosophy. But the Christian should be like Paul, quick to love and show mercy and not breathe out hate and damnation. We should always look at a situation through the eyes of Christ, not through our carnal eye.

Our external ability to make an assessment of someone has two determining factors in our carnal flesh:

(1) How we are feeling that day.
(2) How the other person is feeling that day.

All of us want to be accepted, but few of us are willing to accept others. We all have set barriers around our feelings and emotions, and have preset attitudes toward certain types of people—some of whom we have already condemned to hell.

God has stated that He will supply all of our needs according to His riches in glory. This means we have to be willing to receive what we need. Before we can receive what we need, we need to come to an understanding on what we need. Some may need prayer, others may need hope, and still others may need love. All of these will never measure up to the faith that we all need in God. Without Him we are clueless to understand what we need. However, when we do come into that understanding, we will no longer have broken focus. We will begin to satisfy our need to read.

CHAPTER 11
Is He All the Way in Your Heart?

§

"That He would grant you according to the riches of his glory to be strengthened with might by His Spirit in the inner man; That Christ may dwell in your hearts by faith; that ye being rooted and grounded in love" (*Eph. 3:16–17*).

ANY RELATIONSHIP THAT YOU DESIRE to be long lasting must have commitment, effective communication, and an undying love for the well-being of the other person. Both parties must see the best in life for the other, work diligently to achieve that end, and ensure the courtship of that relationship is always fresh. Now many of you would think I'm talking about a marriage between a man and a woman, but we cannot exclude the relationship between children and their parents, the people on your job, the people in your school, the people in your church, the people in your neighborhood, the people in your family, and even your next-door neighbors.

Paul's revelation is that through the preached gospel, Gentiles—*you and I*—are fellow heirs of the same Christ's body and partakers of God's promises in Christ. When we come to and confess Christ to be the Son of God and our Lord and Savior, as stated in *Ephesians 3:6*, we are endowed with a power that is not of this world. It is interesting how the people of this world are so obsessed with the so-called riches of this world and are not willing to venture and dig deeply into the pages of their Bible to find and claim their eternal inheritance, the true riches of this world. They seek after temporal treasures, wanting temporary treasures, temporary wealth, and temporary prosperity. They are spiritually blind and cannot see the eternal inheritance stored up for them in Christ's kingdom which fare exceeds the wealth of this world.

This thought process has been played out over and over to us for millennia and is now active in our media, our parents, and the church. *"Get yours now"* is the hallmark cry of this age. You don't owe anyone anything. Everyone owes you. Whatever it takes to get it, get it, regardless of whom you hurt in the process. But what are people getting for this motto? Because they have submitted all of their energy to obtaining temporary wealth, they're getting cancer, heart disease, high cholesterol, high blood pressure, gout, and liver disease, just to name a few. All in an attempt to add more stuff to the stuff they already are not using. This age is an age of gatherers. They are not givers, and if they do give, they expect something in return. It is interesting how social media has connected us all by way of the wave, but it now causes us to spend less and less intimate time face-to-face. You don't have to go to church to be in fellowship with the saints anymore. You can stream it. Too many are streaming church services simply because they are too lazy to get up and go. It is too hot or too cold outside so I'll lay here in my comfortable bed and get my praise on. They don't realize that when they hibernate like that, they miss the anointing of the service because they failed to assemble themselves together. They connected with media but missed the intimate connection with the Word. And when this practice becomes habitual, they possess a dead praise simply because they started feeding the desire of their flesh and not the desire of their spirit.

Our social structure has made it possible for you to not make physical eye contact with anyone. You don't have to have face-to-face conversation or confront your issues, your fears, and your concerns in front of a person. You can say what you want to say through media without any regard for the negative impact it may have on the listener or reader, who is clueless to your emotional complaint. Freedom of speech is great, but as *1 Corinthians 10:23* says, "All things are lawful for me, but all things are not expedient (they're not fitting); all things are lawful for me, but all things edify not (they don't educate)."

There is a social all-points bulletin (APB) out for all of the things we didn't know we needed until the person who created the APB had us believe we needed them. They have mastered the art of causing us to believe that once we get it, we can't live without it. Because of this technology, you don't have to let anyone into your personal space. You can keep them in the cloud, and not in Christ. We are *"ever learning but we are not come to the knowledge of truth" (2 Tim. 3:7)*. And for many, when the truth is presented, it is immediately rejected as a lie.

With this approach to life, you can now hide behind your sins. In our mind, we don't have to be naked before anyone, allowing them to see our shortcomings, and we especially don't have to go to God. So many of us have been mentally conditioned to think we can't trust anyone with our feelings and our emotions. It has been said that "women are too petty," and men have the notion that "a man doesn't show his feelings and emotions." Maybe this is the reason why so many are dysfunctional today.

We are too afraid to communicate, too afraid to care, and too afraid to love without reason and without conditions. This is not the plan of God for our lives. It is true that we should not share everything with everyone we develop some type of relationship with, but we can share our testimony. Yes, our sins are our sins, but God has given us someone to help us with overcoming them *and* ourselves. But I also must move past my testimony into a relationship with Jesus. Stop here and read Hebrews 6:1-6. What would cause a person to want to live in their past? Each of us, according to this scripture, have been mandated to leave the foundational things of the gospel and build. We are to build on the foundation and mature in our relationship with God and each other. We are to discard the doctrine of men and pick-up the doctrine of Christ. This Christian journey can't just stop at your belief in Christ, you must accept Him as your savior and my Lord. All of what I'm talking about so far is sin. Each of us must eradicate, remove, erase, and destroy all sin in our lives. We cannot be passive with it. We must pull it up out of us by its root. Before we move on, answer this question: What is the root of your sin?

When we say, "I don't need anyone's help," we give Satan exactly what he wants from us. His whole purpose is to get us to believe that we don't need the spiritual medicine Christ stands ready to give us to heal us from the disease called *sin*. Satan lies to us in an attempt to get us to join his team; and believe it or not, many have. You see, when people get to this state of thinking in their mind garden, their heart becomes hardened, and then they refuse to and cannot receive the truth. God is truth. So, they reject God, and when they reject God, what's left? God said that it is not good for man to be alone. The reason for that is when we spend most of our time alone with our negative thoughts, our emotional issues, and Satan, they begin to control our thinking and ungodly behavior. I hope you caught that. Even when you think you are alone, you have your thoughts. We need one another. Are we so anointed and so deep that we can change the word of God? I don't think so.

God is a relationship God. We were created to have a close relationship with Him. We achieve this by learning day by day how to relate to everyone we come into contact with in the natural, regardless of their disposition. When we make a choice and allow the circumstances of life to separate us from one another in the natural, we unknowingly separate ourselves from God in the spiritual. We will be judged for allowing that natural characteristic of our nature to dominate our spiritual character. When you get a chance, read *Matthew 25:40*.

Do you have the nature of God?

Do you have the character of God?

Do you have the heart of God?

And do you have the mind of God?

The answer to each one of these questions for many today is a resounding *no*! We really want to do better and become better. We don't know how to get there, but God does. He has chosen us to go through His training program of life called time so that we will have the tools to make it into eternity.

Are you *practicing, working, reading, and focusing on* how to *die* to yourself and your sins? This requires some spiritual exercise. Are you in preparation for eternal life? Not many are because that would require some suffering in their flesh and some spiritual exercise. You will have to come out of yourself in order to let Christ in. Like the woman who had the issue of blood (*Matt. 9:20*), our issues are draining the life out of us, and instead of coming to Jesus, we feel like we are missing out on something if we are not carrying them around with us and sharing the story of them with whomsoever will listen. This woman with the issue of blood had no one who wanted to be around her issue. It was the law of the land. As in her case, who do you know that wants to be around your issues every day? And for that matter, name a person you know whose issues you enjoy carrying around with you every day.

God has placed on the inside of you a longing to be close to Him. Satan knows this and is continuously sending weeds, artificial fruit, and lifeless dreams into your mind garden, and if you are not wise in the word of God to fight off these fiery darts, you will willingly give your strength to Satan. If you let him, he will *still* your eternal inheritance from you. He works through others to *destroy* your eternal inheritance, and he will *kill* your desire to pursue your eternal inheritance in God.

How does he do this? He does it with a continuous attack of tribulations and sufferings in your life. His job is to wear you down. He attempts to get you off focus on the prize of the high calling of God in your life (*Phil. 3:14*). He does this by getting you to become prideful or shameful. This is why you can't communicate your perceived God likeness with others. *1 Corinthians 1:26* states: "For ye see your calling, brethren, how that not many wise men after the flesh, not many mighty, not many noble are called." God is not attempting to have a relationship with your flesh. He is seeking a relationship with your inner man—your spirit.

1 Corinthians 7:20–24 reads:

Let every man abide in the same calling in which he was called.

Art thou called, being a servant? Care not for it; but if thou mayest be made free, use it rather.

For he that is called in the Lord, being a servant, is the Lord's freeman; likewise also he that is called being free is Christ's servant.

Ye are bought with a price; but not ye the servants of men.

Brethren, let every man, in whatever state he is called, there abide with God.

That's it! Until we abide with God, we are not giving Christ full access into our hearts. We are not seeking the freedom from this life that only He can give. And as Christ is the husbandman of the church, His work is in our mind soil, to till it and cultivate it in the word of God. Through the word of God, Christ is continuously turning over, tilling and, sifting our mind's dirt to bring us into smooth oneness—complete fellowship with Him. He is the only one who can surgically remove the big and small weeds, the twigs, the stones and the pebbles of destruction from our mind and leave our mind whole in Him—free of disease and sin.

Do you know where you have been rooted? Do you know where you have been grounded? Let's look at Ephesians 3:17. "That Christ may dwell in your hearts by faith; that ye being rooted and grounded in love."

Jesus will only dwell where love is. I don't know of any parent who does not have faith in his or her children's potential. As a matter of fact, if you say the wrong thing to parents about their child or their children, you are subject to find yourself in a fight. Jesus loves us so much that He was willing to die for us. Note: He had to die in order to win. We too must die in order to win. He cares so much for us that He sent the Comforter (the Holy Spirit) to teach and guide us into full fellowship with Him. The deeper our faith, the more rooted we become. The more faith we have, the more grounded we become. *When the affairs of life overcharge us, because we are grounded in the word of God, we don't electrocute the person next to us.* When there is little faith, we open the door for Satan, and we begin to put faith in our sinful nature and not in the righteousness of God. We stop loving. Repeat this to yourself:

I want to be rooted and grounded in Christ.

I want to be fruitful and prosperous and affluent with kingdom things.

I want God to use my gifts and talents for the furtherance of His kingdom.

And I want to be His vessel of praise and worship, with an effective testimony in such a time as this.

All of us must now make the decision to both submit to the call on our lives and gather strength from the Spirit of God to finish this race—or we can go it alone and find ourselves weak in spiritual things and laden with a world of issues. None of us have the strength of the comic book character the Hulk. Remember, his strength is directly in proportion to his anger. *Your strength is in direct proportion to your love.* Love them to life.

What does the word *love* mean to you?

Can you right now think of anything or person that you love more than God? Can you think of anyone that you don't love? *John 13:34–35* reads: "A new commandment I give unto you, that ye love one another as I have loved you, that ye also love one another. By this shall all men know that ye are my disciples, if ye have love one to another."

This is where the rubber meets the road in our lives. How can God expect us to love the people that keep up so much hell in our lives? This is the trillion-dollar question, and it is so easy to answer. How, you ask? I'm glad you did. Let me use myself as the example. I found out that with everyone—and I mean everyone—who comes into the sphere of my influence and puts me into situations that I don't like, I have two choices. I can:

(1) Violently put them in the place I perceive they should be by attacking them in regard to my feelings.
(2) I can be kind and gentle with them, giving them the example of Christ: "Father forgive them for they know not what they do."

Now that is love. What is true for many of us is we don't know what we are doing, we don't know how to love, we haven't had good examples, and we truly have no clue of the negative or positive impact we have on people's lives. And many just don't care.

Jesus cares, however, and He wants us to care. He wants to dwell in us to show us how we should care and how we should love. Care for the sick, care for the naked, care for the lonely, care for the frightened, care for the insecure, care for the needy, care for the rapist, care for the hungry, care for the murderer, care for the homosexual and the lesbian, and care for the weak—just care for mankind. Fathers and mothers should care for their children, but not just for their biological children, but for all children. If you are a stepparent or a guardian over a child's life, you should care. You should care for the people on the job, the people you pass on the street, see in an elevator, at the mall, in your neighborhood store. You should care, and if you care, you should love them and pray:

> Lord, I will glorify thee on the earth; I will finish the work that you gave me to do. I will manifest your name unto everyone I meet. Lord, keep me from the evil one. I am not of this world. Sanctify me in your truth because your word is truth. As you have planted me in the world, show me how to make disciples and sanctify them through your truth. Help me, Father, to become one in you as you and Christ are one. I claim and thank you for the glory that you give me that I may be one with you. Father, the love with which you have loved me, reveal that love through me in all whom I meet that I may be an effective example of your mercy, your grace, and your love.

Today is your day to let Jesus come all the way into your heart, your soul, your strength, and your mind garden. I don't want to frighten you, but we really don't have much time in life here on earth to get it right. Please come on the Lord's side. Receive Christ in your life. Experience the joy and peace only He can bring. I am a living witness to this one fact: Jesus will keep you in perfect peace if you keep your mind stand on Him. He will cultivate your thinking on kingdom things. You will slowly find the things in this world hold no interest for you. Let Jesus fill you with the precious Holy Ghost, who will guide and direct you into the light of Christ. Let Him all the way in—today.

CHAPTER 12
You Are Not Alone

§

He spoke also this parable: A certain man had a fig tree planted in his vineyard; and he came and sought fruit on it, and found none.

Then said he unto the dresser of his vineyard, behold, these three years I come seeking fruit on this fig tree and find none. Cut it down; why cumbereth it the ground?

And he, answering said unto him, Lord, let it alone this year also, till I shall dig about it, and fertilize it;

And if it bear fruit, well; and if not, then after that thou shalt cut it down (*Luke 13:6–9*).

THIS PARABLE OF THE FIG tree is a profound illustration of our condition here on earth. As with this fig tree that was not bearing fruit, many in the church are unaware that they also are not bearing fruit. They are planted in a Bible-believing church. They are planted under an under shepherd who tills their mind soil and feeds them week after week the spiritual nutrients and spiritual fertilizer needed to bring forth a productive harvest of fruit in their lives. But they are not fruitful. As with this tree, no reason is given for their failure to produce, and we would be hard-pressed to pinpoint the cause for the failure of many in the church to produce fruit.

They have the word of God available; they even pray and fast on occasion seeking God's help. But they haven't come to the end of their rope. Let me tell you a fictional story of the plight, the predicament, the dilemma that a young woman whom I will call *Ms. Alone* experienced before she came to Christ.

Ms. Alone married a man who claimed and confessed at the altar that he loved her. He provided for his family and gave his wife everything necessary so that she could make their house a home. In time she gave him three beautiful children, two boys and one girl. Several years further into their marriage was when he began to change. Due to the demands of family life and his job, coupled with a few indiscretions, he eventually left her to raise their three children alone.

Because of his unplanned absence and the suddenness of the transition, she found herself alone and without any income and support to keep food on the table. As a result of this and because she married young and had no marketable skills for a job, she took up prostitution to make ends meet. Do you know anyone like this? As time went on, she began to pray. She hadn't come to know God yet, but she desperately wanted a change in her life and in the lives of her children. For over six months, she visited churches in her surrounding community and eventually joined one. She intimately began to feed on the Word of God and started teaching the things she was learning to her children. In that she started out like the tree in our scripture text, not bearing fruit; she now had begun to bear fruit. She found a job and was able to support her family. She still came across bumps in the road of life, but she now had put her trust completely in the hands of God's promises.

At the beginning of a weekly Bible study at her church, they had a testimony server, and she stood up and thanked God for the changes that had taken place in her life. She testified on all that she went through in order to put all her trust in God and not man. She really felt that she could be transparent with the people in the church.

She immediately found herself being rejected by the women in the congregation. She was rejected because of her past. The women were in awe of her outward beauty and failed to discern the beauty of her inward anointed life in Christ. Her faith caused them to doubt their walk with

God because there were things in their past that had not been confessed. She came to them naked; they came to her like sheep in wolf's clothing.

She also found herself being pursued by single as well as a few of the married men of the congregation. She was being accepted by them as a single woman who had needs. She outwardly was accepted by them for the wrong reason—because of her darkened past. These men had made the church a stalking ground, and every vulnerable woman had become their prey. Let us not get this twisted. There are men who compete with other men of their congregation and other churches for recognition, position, and title. There are also women who stalk the vulnerable men of the church to satisfy their carnal cravings. These cravings are not all related to sex, but the result is the same. A soul is damaged because of a physical lust.

We thank God for the strong biblical foundation set in Ms. Alone's spirit and her love for God. As time went on, she became an effective witness of the love of God to the women in the church, she was able to evangelize the men of the church, and she raised her children up to know God for themselves.

Let each of us be reminded that we are not to judge others. With that judgment, we confess to the world how prideful we are, and we judge ourselves. The Word of God says in *Romans 3:23* that "For all have sinned and come short of the glory of God." Yes, we are born again and are working out our own salvation. *Galatians 6:4* reads: "But let every man judge (prove) his own work, and then shall he have rejoicing in himself alone, and not in another." So many in the church today are quick to judge others and their shortcomings and lacks but fail miserably with fixing the flaws in their own nature and character. In this state, it is hard for one to know their shortcomings and listen to them boast of their total commitment to God. I know you are not perfect; none of us are. But first judge yourself before you open your mouth. Ms. Alone's testimony was a naked confession and a covered-in-the-blood-of-the-Lamb experience. She did not hide her past. She accepted her past, knowing that it set her up for eternal fellowship with her Savior, Jesus Christ, in eternity.

Work

Philippians 2:12b reads: "Work out your own salvation with fear and trembling." Yes! The kingdom-building process requires a lifetime of overtime. There are no days off, there are no holidays, there are no vacations, and there are no breaks. But when we come to the joy of resting in the Lord, it no longer is work; it becomes *the* way to peace and love. It becomes our character. If I truly spent more time working on myself, I would not focus on you. If I spoke more about how my joy comes from the Lord, others would seek to discard the notion that their joy comes from another human being. Again, Ms. Alone was able to do that because she found out that she was not alone. Her existence was not predicated on the physical realm; her existence was predicated wholly on her relationship with God and her sharing and offering that relationship to everyone she met. The word *work* stopped existing in her vocabulary; she had sold out to the joy, the peace, the love, and the fellowship she now had with Jesus Christ. It wasn't physical; it was spiritual—the way it was meant to be when we were created in His image.

What do you think of this story? There are some of you reading this today who may not have prostituted yourself in the way we define prostitution, but you have prostituted yourself. As with this woman, loneliness and the fear for our future has caused many to fall short. Loneliness and the fear for your future can cause you to do things that go against your calling if you let them. When we are not fruitful in the things of God, this means we are barren, we are desolate, and because of this desolation, our minds become cloudy and we don't think clearly. Just like in the natural, when we do not eat regularly, and in many cases if we eat something that doesn't agree with us, we get sick. When we eat continuously at the table of disobedience, we become sick and set up a spiritual infection called sin nature in our lives. We become separated from the presence of God. Because of sin in our lives, people who don't mean us any good can suggest things to us that are not godly, and we sometimes believe and receive what they say. We become fat on disobedience.

Remember, everyone with whom you come into contact, and I mean everyone, is putting up a facade. They are pretending to be something that they are not. There is something about their character that is in hiding. This woman was alone until she found Christ. What she needed, she found out that man could not give it to her. She found out that it wasn't for her to receive anything from anybody in the natural. She found out that everything that she needed could be found in Christ, and only He could take care of her natural needs. She found out that all she had to do was give. She realized that all she had to give to the world was Christ. So many of us are looking for love in all the wrong places. We are afraid to be alone in the natural, and because of this thinking, we allow our minds to be filled with so many weeds of destructive lusts and forget to feed our minds with the word of God. This brings on depression and a mixture of other dysfunctions. So many of us are like this fig true; we are fruitless. The problem is we don't realize we are fruitless; we have just enough of God's word in us to be dangers to our own selves.

Ms. Alone refused to be stuck in her yesterday. So many, however, are. This causes them to not see the potential in their future. This lonely woman, who isn't lonely anymore, could have maintained the spirit of sorrow and become hopelessly sealed in her past, but because of the drawing power of God on her life, she was able to break the chains of despair, break the chains of fear, break the chains of misery, break the chains of loneliness, break the chains of hopelessness, and break the chains of darkness over her life. As in the case with Ms. Alone, each of us must remember this: *No matter how you start this race of life, the object is not for you to come in first place. The object of this race and the object of your life are for you to finish the race, to make it to the finish line. Each day that you quench the fiery darts of Satan, you are a winner. Just finish.*

> And when ye shall come into the land, and shall have planted all manner of trees for food, then ye shall count the fruit thereof as uncircumcised; three years shall it be as uncircumcised unto you; it shall not be eaten.
>
> But in the fourth year all the fruit thereof shall be holy with which to praise the Lord.

And in the fifth year shall ye eat of the fruit thereof that it may yield unto you the increase thereof: I am the Lord your God (*Lev. 19:23–25*).

Some of us are eating uncircumcised fruit. This is because we are uncircumcised. We have not removed our flesh from the equation of life but have made it our center focus. Some of us are eating fruit that is not holy with which to praise the Lord. Some of us are eating fruit that has no ability to yield an increase in our lives. We have not allowed the Spirit of God to dig around our inner man and fertilize the garden of our mind with love so that the fruit that is to spring forth from our bellies can feed the family of God.

Ms. Alone had three children. Now we all know that a day can be a thousand years with the Lord and a year can be a day. Her three children represent the years of her being uncircumcised with her husband. She operated in her flesh. When she made the decision, when she became determined to put God first in her life, her life changed. Even though she was not mature enough in the word of God, she began to mature by not focusing on the flesh; more and more she focused on the word of God.

Her willingness to continue to love her husband even though he mistreated her, to forgive those in the church who failed to walk in Christ, and to be an effective witness to all brought her into her eighth day. When she entered into her eighth day, she received her fruitful increase and a new beginning. Note that her increase was not monetary; it wasn't about money. Her increase was her testimony, her time in the wilderness. The seeds of the Holy Ghost that she planted in her children and her praise and worship of God all brought her into her ninth day and produced a harvest of souls for the kingdom of God. She became an example of a good and faithful steward. Anyone who listened to her would know that God had made a change in her life. All of those individuals that she was acquainted with before Christ also had a testimony of the change in her life. And a few were drawn to Him.

Somebody out there today—some child, some man, some woman—you need to know that the day you turned your life over to Christ and surrendered your past and your present to Him, He gave you everything you need to be the salt of the earth, the light on the hill, right now. Everyone that comes into contact with you receives a taste of the love and peace God seeded in your life through your walk and in your speech. God has given you everything you need to be the light of the world. Your conversations turn a dark situation into a bright display of joy and hope. Your correct use of your spiritual gifts is bringing forth an increase into the kingdom of God. Even now God is sending spiritual fertilizer into your life so that you may absorb those spiritual nutrients needed for your spiritual roots to dig deep into the soil of the word of God so that you can bear more fruit and move to the next level in God. Life eternal.

Some of us, however, have not matured enough yet, but know this: We are yet maturing in our faith, we are maturing in our love for God, and we are maturing in our love for others. Some of us in the church just pursue fellowship only with those in the church. If you have family members who are lost, you have left it up to someone else to witness to them, forgetting that you are either to plant seed or water the seed that has been planted.

Ms. Alone was lost. God began to draw her to Himself and she surrendered everything about herself to Him. She did not dwell in her past. She did not break under her present condition. She began to see a better future—a future that was filled with the presence of Christ, her Savior and her Lord.

What is your spiritual calling in the kingdom of God? If you don't know what your call is, you need to find out today. We all must be careful in these last days. So many distractions, so many temptations are attempting to take our focus off our purpose in building the kingdom of God. We must be willing to not just have a testimony; *we must sacrifice our flesh in order to become the testimony.* Many will attempt to belittle you, some will ignore you while others will discard you, but there are a few who will connect with you. Remember, Jesus had seventy of his disciples leave Him because they could not separate the physical from the natural. He said we were to eat His body and drink His blood. As we become one with Him, we are His body, and we are His blood. We too have been and are being poured out into the world to call others into repentance so they can have the joy that we have. The kingdom of God is at hand. The kingdom of God should be in you, and if it is in you, its roots should be spreading outside of you and impacting the lives of everyone you come into contact with. To some your impact will be positive; to others your impact will be negative. This isn't your focus. Your focus should be, in love, to just *impact*! Always impacting for the kingdom of God.

Starting today and for the rest of your life here on this earth, you will become more and more circumcised for the Lord. You will want every bit of your flesh to be cut away, and you will want to die in Christ so that His Spirit can have free rein in and over your life as He lives in you. Ask God to make the fruit of your life to be holy and acceptable to Him. You then will begin to enjoy the fruits of your labor for the kingdom.

I am humbled today to know beyond a shadow of a doubt that there is someone who loves me even when I fall short of my potential and sometimes don't love myself. God believes in me even when I don't believe in myself. As we end this chapter, say this to yourself: *"I thank God that I am not alone!"*

CHAPTER 13
Don't Play the Fool

The fool hath said in his heart, there is no God. They are corrupt, they have done abominable works, there is none that doeth good.

The Lord looked down from heaven upon the children of men to see if there were any that did understand and seek God.

They are all gone aside, they are all together become filthy. There is none that doeth good, no not one.

Have all the workers of iniquity no knowledge? Who eat up my people as they eat bread and call not upon the Lord?

There were they in great fear: for God is in the generation of the righteous (*Ps. 14:1–5*).

THIS PASSAGE OF SCRIPTURE IS a statement of fact. The whole race of man had left God and the straight path and chose the crooked path. They have become morally deficient. The denial of God is the first step in total apostasy (*Rom. 1:21–32*). When one loses faith in God, he or she gradually sinks into the depraved life of the ungodly. They lose faith and respect for each other. In this text we find several steps that reveal the path to church abandonment and backsliding:

1. Ignore God
2. Heart darkened
3. Living foolishly

4. Serve creature more than the Creator
5. Does not seek God
6. Live with perverted affections
7. Accepts a lie and rejects the truth
8. Lives a filthy lifestyle
9. Shows no understanding
10. Mistreats God's people
11. Never talks to God
12. Disrespects the poor

I have not found anyone that enjoys and likes being called a fool. This is because we all want to be recognized for our self-worth; we want to be accepted, and we want to fit in. No matter our perceived worth or the worth others try to categorize us in, we want to feel a part of something, and for that very reason, some will not choose the knowledge of good; they will instead pursue the knowledge of evil. Evil will accept anything that you want to do. God will not. Civil law will accept anything you want to do. God will not.

The knowledge of good and evil is described as a tree in *Genesis 2:9*. It is pleasant to the sight and good for food; see also *Genesis 3:6*. This means that this tree bore fruit. Before we can go any further, I want you to note that sin is always at the door of our mind garden when we want to partake of something that isn't good for us at the time. Not all fruit is good for us. God will always know what is best for us *right now* to consume. In many cases our *right now* isn't the best time to consume the fruit we see. In the garden, because man was not ready to deal with evil and take dominion over it, God warned him of the impact it would have on his life if he partook of it—death. Without any regard for God's warning of the consequences of his action, Adam succumbed; he submitted to it, and it took dominion over him. Sin corrupted his soul nature. When we are not wholly submitting to God—who is pure goodness—we unknowingly submit ourselves to Satan, who is pure evil. As Adam and Eve found out, there is no in-between.

When we realize that we have participated in any of the above twelve mentioned apostasies, we find a way, in our own thinking, to justify the behavior. It will always be someone else's fault for our actions. But when the apostasy is done against us, we call foul play and turn right around and commit apostasy against the person that committed it against us. Again, we justify our actions, but two wrongs don't equal a right. This behavior is proof that we have not died to self. We get attitudes with one another, we disrespect one another, we fight one another, and in some cases, we kill one another over a perceived offense. In some cases the person doing the offending isn't aware of it. The reason I say this is because all of us have different life experiences, which are predicated on our limited ability to think clearly; we speak and act in ways that are comfortable only to us.

Have you ever noted how someone else's behavior can offend you? It is sad, however, because you need to come to the realization that some of your behaviors are also offensive. Offense is not a characteristic of God, and it should not be a characteristic of His children. There are two primary reasons one may become offended:

(1) He doesn't know who he is.
(2) He feels that someone has disrespected the identity he believes is himself.

In either example, the root of the offense is centered on self. Self is your enemy, not the individual. When you operate in self, you operate in the natural. Again, this earth is cursed, which makes your sin nature a curse. Nothing done in the natural will come to a positive end. We were created in the image and likeness of God. *Only what is done in the image and likeness of God can bring life.*

In Jesus's sermon on the mount (*Matt. 5:22*), He says, "But I say unto you that whosoever is angry with his brother without a cause shall be in danger of the judgment; and whosoever shall say to his brother, Raca (worthless) shall be in danger of the council: but whosoever shall say, thou fool shall be in danger of hell fire."

Everyone should know that anger and rage are the first steps toward committing murder. If not in the physical, it can occur psychologically. They are the opposite of grace and mercy, and they open the mind to hate, and hate opens the mind to destructive behavior. When we talk negatively about anyone, we murder that person's character in the mind of the person we share our anger with. We tend to not want to come off like we are angry with the person, so we make it sound like an observation of fact. Here is the sad part of this act: We never went to the person we are talking about, in love, to address our feelings and emotions on the action he or she took. We allowed the enemy, Satan, to plant seeds of destruction in our mind garden, and we spread those seeds to whoever would listen. Just as God will judge our love and tender mercy toward others, be assured that He will also judge our anger, our quarrelsome speech, and our hate toward others. When we get to the point that we regard one person to be better than another—or less than another—we commit murder. Too often we quarrel and hold hostilities toward a person because we feel more worthy or less worthy than that person. So Jesus tells us that whatsoever we do to the least of our brothers, we do it also to Him. Regardless of what your status is in life, we all stand equal in the eyes of Christ.

Our court system deals with the act of a crime; *God deals with the root cause of a crime.* No one wants to accept the reality that there is a demonic nature in all humans. Don't forget: We were born in sin and shaped in iniquity. We can truthfully be called children of God only when we are born again, turn to God in repentance, and claim our deliverance from our hell-bound nature. We must be born again. The council of man wants justice. The council of God, however, is *mercy* and *grace*. Each born-again believer is to exhibit these attributes of God—mercy and grace. Be quick to forgive and slow to pass judgment. Be quick to restore and slow to cast out. We are to leave all judgment to God, for we don't know the final outcome of a person's life, we don't know the end of his or her story, and we definitely don't know God's plan for a person's life. Who do you have a grudge against right now? *Repent* before it is too late. We are all brothers because we are children of God, and for those that claim sonship in God, *you have been called to die to yourself in Christ so that the lost – dead in their sin souls – can be led to Christ by your life witness and sacrifice.*

Hellfire is a place where the worm never dies and the fire is never quenched. None of us can call anyone a fool because to make that statement toward an individual's character catapults us toward the dangerous door of hellfire, for we become the fool. The nature of God does not quarrel or argue back and forth. It is alien to God and should be alien to each of us. When we allow ourselves to get to the point in our anger and our quarrelsome nature toward a brother that we can call him a fool, be assured that we have moved into a complete worship of ourselves. Self is the real fool here today. It is self that not only separates us from one another, but self also separates itself from God—*its life source*. As I stated earlier, a **s**elfish **i**ndividual **n**ature (*sin*) has alienated us from God. It will alienate you from your family, and it will alienate you from the family of God. This is why getting saved from your sins and being born again in your spirit is so crucial to your Christlikeness. That foolish nature has to die, and you must repent.

> "To whom ye forgive anything, I forgive also; for if I forgive anything, to whom I forgive it, for your sake forgive I it in the person of Christ. Lest Satan should get an advantage of us; for we are not ignorant of his devices (*2 Cor. 2:10–11*).

In all the suffering of mind, heart, and body—afflictions, anguish, beating, distress, fasting, fighting, labors, perils, persecution, sorrow, stripes, sufferings, tears, disorder, weak, and weakness—of Paul, he failed not to give God glory for them all. Note that these are all events that take place in the flesh, including your mind garden—your thoughts. Regardless of our stature and ranking in life, life assures all of us the opportunity to experience at least one, if not all, of the above-stated sufferings. Who is excluded from this? *No one!*

Each of us then should have the spirit of forgiveness, and with the spirit of forgiveness, we should have the spirit of reconciliation. Just because someone does not do things the way you would do them does not make you wrong or right, and it does not make him or her wrong or right. It does, however, show the differences that two individuals coming from two separate backgrounds and life experiences have. It shows how two people from separate life experiences and two different domestic backgrounds may perceive a solution to a particular issue and their approach to bringing a resolve.

I have heard it said that we should *find our place, get in our place, work in our place, and stay in our place.* When we don't follow this blueprint, we tend to find someone else's place, we get into someone else's place, we work in someone else's place, and we want to stay in someone else's place. I cannot walk your road called straight. You cannot walk my road called straight, and we all should know that we cannot walk two roads at the same time.

I don't want to sound repetitive, but this world is coming to an end. You will continuously hear me make this statement because it is true and I don't believe many are convinced of this fact. It is not an attempt to frighten you. It is an attempt to remind you that we are to watch and pray. Each of us must make up in our mind to esteem others higher than ourselves. *Philippians 2:3* reads: "Let nothing be done through strife or vainglory, but in lowliness of mind let each esteem others better than themselves." The door of humility has a key that has been broken off in the door of the church. The part of the key that was held in our heart has been lost. It has been discarded, and in some churches, it has been thrown away. The broken-mechanism part of the key is stuck in the door, and no one is able to use it to open the door. Some of you took this statement to refer to the church building. This statement refers to you, for you and I are the church building, the body of Christ. *We all have to go on bended knees before God to find the broken key of humility.* We have to learn how to accept humiliation without retaliation. We have to suffer and thank God for that suffering, for it will present to us a great opportunity to be an effective witness for the gospel of Christ.

When we find the broken key, each of us individually must give it to the Holy Spirit and let Him unlock the door so the seeds of humility can be planted in our mind garden. If we unlock it, we will operate in pride. When He unlocks it, we will operate in praise. When the seeds of humility begin to germinate in our mind garden, they will produce a wanting to understand our brother and our sister—and not an overwhelming desire to be understood. Know this: God understands. You will begin to have tolerance of those that are different than you. You will begin to seek opportunities to give and not receive, and you will want to promote the life of Christ into the life of all you meet. Your born-again lifestyle will become a beacon of light to everyone around you. People who don't know you will hear of your tender love and mercy toward others.

You will come out of your physical church building and take the church—yourself—to the worlds you live in, first in your mind garden, and then to all the mind gardens you have opportunity to witness to: your church, your job, your home, your social gatherings, and even your enemies. Every thought that you have will be a thought to witnessing the good news of Jesus Christ. You will find yourself honoring everyone and thanking God for your differences. Don't be afraid. Let the light of Christ shine in you and out of you. Let your words bring the healing balm for the souls that cross your path daily. Let Christ reign in your mind garden, and you will find yourself reigning in His kingdom.

> To them who by patient continuance in well-doing seek for glory and honor and immortality, eternal life;
>
> But unto them that are contentious (argumentative, combative), and do not obey the truth, but obey unrighteousness, indignation and wrath,
>
> Tribulation and anguish upon every soul of man that doeth evil, of the Jew first and also of the Greek (*Rom. 2:7–9*). All men without exception who live without faith in Christ are lost.

Too often when we come into the knowledge of good, we claim it for ourselves. We have knowledge but we don't have an understanding. Everything that we do, what we say, and how we live are centered on our belief of what good is. After a few short weeks of acceptance and recognition by others, we unknowingly become god idols in our own imagination and believe that all that we do, all that we say, and how we live is the answer for everyone who we allow to grace our presence. Our way becomes the only way.

Paul is warning us of this. Well-doing must line up with the life and perfect will of Christ. Well-doing is directly in line with doing God's will. If we are to teach, if we are to preach, our lives must be an example of Christ. Can anyone say that he or she lives the life of Christ? I will be bold and say, *no*! Even in our confessed born-again state, we fall short. But the issue here is not in the falling short. The issue here is your attitude toward your shortfall. What you do immediately after you realize you have slipped, tripped or fallen. Do you waddle in it allowing Satan to feed you more weeds, or do you stand up, repent and walk away.

God's sons and daughters are to emulate the example of Christ, and when we don't, we become worthless and valueless in winning souls to Christ; we become fools. Let us take time right now and examine ourselves. Let us examine the motives of our actions. Let us allow the Holy Spirit to put us on the spiritual operating table of deliverance and surgically remove all carnal weeds of pride from our garden. When we submit to Him, He will stand up in us and for us. *We do not have to play the fool any longer.*

CHAPTER 14
Just A.S.K.

§

"So I say to you: Ask and it will be given to you; seek and you will find; knock and the door will be opened to you (*Luke 11:9*).

JESUS SPEAKS THESE WORDS ALSO in *Matthew 7:7–8*: "Ask and it will be given to you; seek and you will find; knock and the door will be opened to you."

This revelation that Jesus brings to us is to be applied like an ointment to every area of our thinking. As His disciples, His brothers and sisters, and as the sons and daughters of God, we are to saturate ourselves in this truth. That truth is the fact that God is the supplier of all of our needs. He is not the supplier of our wants, and if we cannot differentiate between the two, if we cannot distinguish and discern the desires of God's heart toward what He has planned for us versus our plans for our lives, we will have a problem with God. In His infinite wisdom, God created all that we would need before He created us. He created the planet for us to live on, He created the atmosphere for us to breathe, He created water for us to drink, and He created food for us to eat. He didn't leave out anything. Yet, *we want more!*

Previously in the tenth chapter of Luke, Jesus had sent seventy of His disciples out to preach that the kingdom of God had come near unto them. He told these disciples to carry no money, no bag, and no shoes and to greet no man by the way. They were to carry only the clothes on their backs. These men were expecting an immediate end, for they thought the end of the world would come in their lifetime. The urgency and seriousness of their message is indicated here in that they were not to indulge in unnecessary conversations, on their journey. They were to embrace their assignment with their whole person. It became the purpose for their existence. This attitude should be the purpose for our existence as well.

Some in the ministry of this generation do not feel this urgency, and it has caused many to become unfaithful and lazy in their Christian walk. They have lost their ability to be effective witnesses. Wherever the gospel is preached, "the Kingdom of God is near," and each soul is given a choice. People can choose life, or they can choose death. They can choose heaven, or they can choose hell.

Now when the seventy disciples returned to Jesus, they returned with joy, saying, "Lord, even the devils—demons are subject unto us through thy name." Because their cares for their lives were transformed from a natural need to a spiritual need, these seventy disciples were able to pull down the strongholds of darkness in the lives of everyone who would hear them and believe them while on that journey. This was possible due to the urgency of their message and the anointing placed on them by Christ. Just let me add: *Each of us is on a journey, and we too should be anointed in Christ to evangelize the hurting and the lost.*

Something happens to us as we transition from childhood to adulthood. We lose that inquisitive mind. We become all-knowing and stop asking questions. Children want to know *why* things are like they are. Their minds are like a sponge, ready to absorb everything their parents and their environment tells and shows them. When they don't understand, they follow the conversation with another question, which is the same question: *Why?* As a child, we are not able to connect one idea with another idea and build a word picture of understanding and complete thought. We wear our parents out with that word for two reasons. The first reason is because they don't know how to give us a comprehensible answer at our level of comprehension. The second reason is that in some instances, we lost interest in the answer because we allowed our mind to wander.

Let me take a few minutes to break down each of these *present imperatives*: *ask*, *seek*, and *knock*. Each of them is a necessary tool on your Christian journey.

Don't Bite the Distraction

The first present imperative is *ask*. When we ask people for something, we are calling on them for an answer. We call on them for the answer because we don't have the answer and we believe that they have enough knowledge and life experience to give us an answer that we can accept. When Satan entered the garden, the first thing he did was ask a question: *"Yea, hath God said...?" (Gen. 3:1).* His attempt was to cast doubt in the tender mind of Eve. He caused her to have uncertainty and to hesitate in her thinking. She may have even questioned what her husband had said to her. This event should let us know that there are some questions that are designed to trick and to manipulate our thinking and we should not entertain them.

All of our questions can be answered if we would just spend more quality time reading and studying our Bible. God is so eager to reveal Himself to us, but like I said earlier, so many are not willing to gather the basic information about Him in order to come to the right conclusion, a deeper understanding of the truth of His power. We are receiving so much mental stimuli when we are awake and when we are asleep. Coupled with our dreams, we can have a mental overload. The child who asks the question "Why?" wants to know, but he or she hasn't received enough information to truly understand. In many cases, children are asking questions just to hear themselves talk. If we are not careful with the level of information we give them predicated on their ability to absorb the information (pay attention) and make sense of it (understand), we can be the cause of not only their distraction, but more importantly, their destruction.

God is always presenting to us all the information regarding Himself and His relationship with us. This is why He put together a blueprint for us, the Bible. From this blueprint, He reveals to us how to build a relationship with Him and with others. He opens up our opportunities to experience His love and makes known how much He wants to supply our every need. You see, Satan asked a question to Eve, but God asked a question to Adam in *Genesis 3:9*: *"Where art thou?" Satan's question questioned God's authority. God's question questioned man's position.*

This lets us know that whenever we find ourselves entertaining a question given to us by Satan, we open the door for ourselves to operate in the flesh, we are in the wrong position. When we are out of position we question God. God wants us to question ourselves. Where are you? This is a right now question. Try it! Ask yourself, *"Where am I right now?"* We must live in the right now. Where are you right now? Where are your thoughts right now? Are you constantly thinking of your past failures, are you sitting in the seat of indecisiveness, or are you stuck in both of them unable to move into your destiny? Wherever you are right now, you need to believe that God has your answer. You must ask the right question: "Who am I?" And answer it with: "I am a child of God." "What is my purpose?" To worship Him and serve Him. "How do I serve Him?" I serve Him by esteeming others higher than myself and leading the lost to Him. This is how you take dominion of your mind garden. As you read and study the word of God each day, His spirit will give you all the answers you need to die to yourself and live in him.

The Truth and Nothing But the Truth

The next *present imperative* is *seek*. Let me ask one questions here. What are you seeking? The answer for many would be different. Some are seeking more money, some are seeking more recognition, some are seeking peace of mind, others are seeking a title, while there are a few that are seeking the opportunity to be left alone. Out of all of the seeking that we do, it is sad how we have failed to seek one thing, and if we seek it, we seek it to justify ourselves. That is the truth. God's truth should hold a great interest in our thinking. It is the one thing we all should be seeking.

Truth is most often used to mean being in accord with fact or reality, or fidelity to an original or to a standard or ideal. Many people today have their own opinion of a fact, their own truth that has nothing to do with God. Many illnesses and diseases were believed to be caused by one thing or another until our ability in the science of medicine; the study of cells and organisms, we found that foods prepared improperly can cause suffering. Even the study in mental health has opened our minds to a deeper truth of our emotional condition. Everything about us reveals the truth of God. Everything in nature reveals the truth of God, and everything on earth and in the seas reveals the truth of God. But Satan asked one question that has caused many to doubt God's truth. Believe it or not, this is how mental illness entered into the earth realm. Find a soul that has no God and you will find Satan working great destruction in that person's life; thus, with his work, mental illness and physical infirmity are increasing.

Can you imagine what the church could do if she received her husband, respected her husband, honored her husband, and understood her role as His bride? When the church stopped seeking the truth, when she stopped hearing truth spoken to her by her husband, when she set out to do her own thing, what she did, unbeknown to her, she divorced Christ. Not only did she divorce Him, He who gives life, but she began to seek after him who gives death and began to bear his children. She could no longer hear, she could no longer see, and she could no longer witness to Christ's tender love for her. She now finds herself spiritually hemorrhaging and slowly losing her assets in large amount. Like the woman who had the issue of blood in *Luke 8:3–48*, not only was she unable to reproduce kingdom children, but she found herself alone; no one wanted to be around her. She had to yell out *"unclean"* when she came into close contact with people. Just look at the world's response to the church today. She doesn't have to call herself unclean; the world calls her unclean.

More than ever before in history, the church has found herself having to yell out to the world, *"unclean,"* and this is because she, like Eve, did not answer Satan with the scripture but answered him out of her own earthly desires. As you can see, when we don't respond to this world with the word of God, we are subject to seek the wrong things.

Check Your Imagination at the Door

Our third and final *present imperative* is *knock*. Knocking denotes that we are attempting to gain entry into and through a door. Life has many doors waiting for us to enter in. Some are unlocked, some are jammed, and others are locked. The condition of the door really doesn't make a difference; what should be important to us is what is behind the door. Some doors are beautifully crafted with precious metals and stones. Looking at them you would think more precious items are behind them. Other doors have a refined look. These doors show potential. They have an educated look about them that is not barbaric. And then there are doors that seem so common that you could mistake them for something other than a door.

This is where the wisdom of God comes into play. God never attempts to get our attention with what seems beautiful, what seems refined, and what seems common. He will only present to us the door of truth. Our own imagination will fill in the blanks. You see, we sometimes don't have to knock on the door. We need to listen for His knock on the door so that we will know which door to open so we can let Him in. He is always knocking on the door of our heart. He desires access so that He can mend our broken heart. We have become so used to our broken hearts that we imagine that we are just fine. We think we don't need to answer His knock—but we do. He is the only physician that can fix us.

Yes, it is better to give than to receive. Jesus gave His life, and He is asking us to obey, He is seeking for those who will receive Him, and He is knocking on our hearts wanting access. When He gives, we are to receive. He gives eternal life, and we receive eternal life from Him. The only thing that we have to give is ourselves, and oh how painful that can be. He has called us to Him and stands ready to supply all of our needs.

Take a few minutes and look inside yourself and determine what you want. Trust me, if you can name one thing that you want that is in the natural, you are close to missing God. What am I saying? I'm saying that when all of your wants conclude with giving your complete self to God, then and only then can He trust you with the desires of your heart because as He gives to you, you will give toward the building of His kingdom. Did you catch that? He wants to give you the tools to build His kingdom. As you begin to gather more and more tools for the building of His kingdom, you will begin to gather more and more territory for the kingdom-building process. You will desire to gather souls for the kingdom, and you will be willing to lay down your life for the furtherance of His kingdom.

Everything about you will be directed to His kingdom, not your independent tribe. You will envision the massiveness of His kingdom and will give up your tribe of ideas and emotions in order to obtain the territory He has already prepared for you. You will no longer be working yourself to death; you will be working yourself to life and that more abundantly.

The reason that each of us should be asking, seeking, and knocking is because we really should want to know our kingdom assignment. Do you know yours? God is waiting for you to come to Him so that He can instruct and direct you into your purpose; so that you can fulfill your assigned destiny. In order to fulfill your destiny, you must be obedient and not a complainer. The reason Jesus's body could not be recognized on the cross was because He had been wiped and beat into an unrecognizable fleshly form. How does the world recognize you? Is it because of your carnal nature, or is it because of your spiritual anointed suffering nature that is unrecognizable to the world? Each of us must drink of our own afflictions as we die to this world's devices. Only then can we complete our earthly assignment and place our soul into the hand of God. Yes, you read it correctly; you must willingly place your soul into the healing hand of God and allow His Spirit to minister to your spirit. He will revive you in a praise and worship revival, causing you to put all of your trust in Him and not in the flesh of the world.

It's Your Choice. It's Your Will.

As I prepare to close this chapter, let me stress that each of us is in training for eternity. The question then is: Where do you want to spend eternity? In the light of God's kingdom, or chained under the darkness of Satan's kingdom? To each question we A.S.K., we should respond with an answer that teaches us how to come out of darkness and causes us to focus more on the light of Jesus Christ. The one thing that we should be seeking is that road, that street called straight, that equips us with the necessary tools for building God's kingdom on earth—our mind. The door that we should knock on is the door to our heart, for it is the stoniness of our heart that needs to be broken up; the hand of God needs to perform spiritual surgery and give us a Christ like heart and a spiritual blood transfusion.

Luke 11:13 reads: "If ye then being evil know how to give good gifts unto your children, how much more shall your heavenly Father give the Holy Spirit to them that ask Him?"

It is the Holy Spirit and only the Holy Spirit that can lead us into all truth. It is the Holy Spirit who can strengthen our faith; it is the gift of the Holy Spirit that gives us the power to have all of our needs met, all of our sickness removed, and our faith and trust in God restored. If you today are still operating in the power of your spirit, tell me the level of your success to receive peace, love, and joy. It is only through the power of the Holy Spirit that we can put the cares of this world kingdom behind us. God is looking for a holy people, and all we have to do to obtain holiness is to ask for Him, seek Him, and when He knocks at the door of our heart, let Him in. He will take over from there. Just A.S.K. When He comes, *let Him in*.

CHAPTER 15
Spiritual Warfare—Your Armor

§

TODAY IS THE DAY WE begin to take Satan's kingdom down in the minds of our loved ones, our friends, and our enemies, and in our own lives.

There is a situation that many of us are experiencing with combating sin in our lives. It is a *multidimensional* sin issue as discussed in *Dr. Edward F. Murphy's* book titled *The Handbook for Spiritual Warfare*. He states that as Christian soldiers, we continually combat evil on three fronts: the *flesh*, the *world*, and the *devil*. We do so in hopes that some can be snatched out of hell, while others will choose to die to the lure of the flesh, the lure of the world, and the lure of the devil, and follow Christ.[1]

As we begin this chapter, it is imperative that we saturate the battleground—our mind—with prayer and with scripture. It will be just as important for us to fast. You see, these three spiritual weapons when used for the glory of the kingdom of God, will enable you to be an overcomer. The objects of destruction that you must overcome are yourself, your flesh, and the things of this world that you have allowed your flesh to become addicted to. *We are going to work through and destroy family generation curses. We will move you into identifying your spiritual gifts and how to walk in them.* Let's look at *Matthew 17:14–21*. It tells a story of the powerless disciples. *Is it talking about you?* Let's read:

And when they were come to the multitude, there came to Him a certain man kneeling down to him and saying.

Lord, have mercy on my son for he is lunatic [epileptic] and greatly vexed for often he falls into the fire and often into the water.

And I brought him to your disciples and they could not cure him.

Then Jesus answered and said, O faithless and perverse generation, how long shall I be with you? How long shall I suffer with you? Bring him here to me.

And Jesus rebuked the demon and he departed out of him and the child was cured from that very hour.

Then came the disciples to Jesus privately and said, why could not we cast him out?

And Jesus said unto them, because of your unbelief; for verily I say unto you, if ye have faith as a grain of mustard seed, ye shall say unto this mountain *move* from here to yonder place and it shall move and nothing shall be impossible unto you.

Howbeit this kind goeth not out but by prayer and fasting.

Many of us have attempted to rid ourselves of the issues in our flesh with no success. This father attempted for at least twelve years to rid his son of his condition with no success, but when he met Jesus, his son's life changed for the better.

Jesus is waiting to empower and to inspire you to become born again in your spirit. He will change your thinking and free you from the addiction of your flesh. Like this child, we often fall into fires and get burned, and we often fall into deep waters and nearly drown, but by the grace of God, we are still here. Jesus wants each of us to know that we do not have to burn and we do not have to drown. We are not to climb mountains; we are to move them out of our way. We must have a strong prayer life and a stronger life of fasting. We then will die to our fleshly addictions, rise above every condition of darkness, and walk a life centered in the light of Christ. In the church today however, prayer and fasting are curse words to the Christian. We can come to church and worship and praise for an hour. We can go to Christian concerts and do the same. But when it comes to developing a strong fasting and prayer life there are very few who even attempt the practice. If you have not developed a strong fasting and prayer life, be assured that you are catering to the desires of your flesh and not to the needs of your spirit man. The best way to fertilize your spiritual mind is through fasting and prayer. Just as your physical body is always in need of physical nutrients, your spiritual roots are always in need of spiritual nutrients. If we are honest with ourselves right now, we feed our natural man more then we feed our spiritual man. As Jesus told his disciples, we are perverse. We are willfully determined or disposed to go counter to what is expected or desired of us by God.

This is what *Deuteronomy 31:29* says about us: "For I know that after my death ye will utterly corrupt yourselves and turn aside from the way which I have commanded you, and evil will befall you in the latter days because you will do evil in the sight of the Lord to provoke him to anger through the work of your hands."

This is what Moses said to the congregation of elders and officers of the twelve tribes of Israel just before they entered the Promised Land. Just as God had warned Moses of the apostasy of His people, He reminds us too of our own apostasy toward Him. Each of us is either an elder in the congregation of our family, or we are an officer in our church, in our home, or on our job. God knows our heart, and it is wicked. There is no getting around it. We are at war with an enemy that does not take prisoners—ourselves. *Yes, without Christ, you are an enemy to yourself.* You have to ask God for insight, foresight, and discernment. What looks good through your fleshly eyes could be the wolf in sheep's clothing. Trust me, Satan knows your weaknesses. He knows them better than you.

As we learn of our own wickedness, we will gather tools to cut it out of our lives. Remember, these wicked behaviors are our addictions, and there will be some major withdrawal from them. But rest assured that when it is all over, you will know that Satan has lost, and you are no longer the victim; you are the victor. Get ready for the battle of your life.

WHAT DO YOU SEE?

Isaiah 65:17 states: "For behold, I create heavens and a new earth and the former shall not be remembered, nor come into mind."

Luke 17:20–21 states: "And when he was demanded of the Pharisees when the kingdom of God should come, He answered them and said, 'The kingdom of God cometh not with observation. Neither shall they say, Lo here! Or lo there! For behold, the kingdom of God is within you."

Don't you want the awesome light of God's kingdom to dwell and shine within you and through you? Don't you want to be born again? Don't you want to be filled with God's Spirit? Jesus is standing at the door of your heart right now, and all you have to do is open your heart to Him. Today is the day for you to obtain the spiritual weaponry needed to protect your soul from the fiery darts of the wicked one and place a hedge of protection around those you love. God said, "Let there be light," in *Genesis 1:3*. Why was there a need for light? I don't know of any human being that is nocturnal. Unless you are in the military or are a hunter who has night-vision glasses, you are blind at night. God wants our vision to be clear. He wants us to see what He sees. This cannot happen when we walk in darkness. Satan was the angel of light (*2 Cor. 11:14*), but he chose to walk in darkness. Satan does not want you to see. His mission is to keep you in darkness and far away from the light of God. Some have been in darkness for so long that the saints will have to work in shifts in order to adjust their vision to be able to receive light. When a heart has been darkened by the words and darts of Satan, that soul fears the light and light becomes their enemy. Our job is to win them, to sacrifice everything we have so that they can come to the penetrating light of God's love and live.

The lord is my light and my salvation; whom shall I fear? The Lord is the strength of my life; of whom shall I be afraid?

When the wicked, even mine enemies and my foes, came upon me to eat up my flesh, they stumbled and fell.

Though an host should encamp against me, my heart shall not fear; though war should rise against me, in this will I be confident.

One thing have I desired of the Lord, that will I seek after: that I may dwell in the house of the Lord all the days of my life, to behold the beauty of the Lord, and to inquire in his temple.

For in the time of trouble he shall hide me in his pavilion; in the secret of his tabernacle shall he shade me; he shall set me up upon a rock.

And now shall mine head be lifted up above mine enemies round about me. Therefore will I offer in his tabernacle sacrifices of joy; I will sing, yea, I will sing praises unto the Lord.

Hear, O Lord, when I cry with my voice; have mercy also upon me, and answer me.

When thou sadist, Seek ye my face, my heart said unto thee, Thy face, Lord, will I seek.

Hide not thy face far from me; put not thy servant away in anger. Thou hast been my help; leave me not, neither forsake me, O God of my salvation.

When my father and my mother forsake me, then the Lord will take me up.

Teach me thy way, O Lord, and lead me in a plain path, because of mine enemies.

Deliver me not over unto the will of mine enemies; for false witnesses are risen up against me, and such as breathe out cruelty.

I had fainted, unless I had believed to see the goodness of the Lord in the land of the living.

Wait on the Lord; be of good courage, and he shall strengthen thine heart. Wait, I say, on the Lord. (*Psalms 27:1-14*)

Give ear to my prayer, O God; and hide not thyself from my supplication.

Attend unto me, and hear me: I mourn in my complaint, and make a noise,

Because of the voice of the enemy, because of the oppression of the wicked: for they cast iniquity upon me, and in wrath they hate me.

My heart is sore pained within me: and the terrors of death are fallen upon me.

Fearfulness and trembling are come upon me, and horror hath overwhelmed me.

And I said, Oh that I had wings like a dove! For then would I fly away, and be at rest.

Lo, then would I wander far off, and remain in the wilderness. Selah.

I would hasten my escape from the windy storm and tempest.

Destroy, O Lord, and divide their tongues: for I have seen violence and strife in the city.

Day and night they go about it upon the walls thereof: mischief also and sorrow are in the midst of it.

Wickedness is in the midst thereof: deceit and guile depart not from her streets.

For it was not an enemy that reproached me; then I could have borne it: neither was it he that hated me that did magnify himself against me; then I would have hid myself from him:

But it was thou, a man mine equal, my guide, and mine acquaintance.

We took sweet counsel together, and walked unto the house of God in company.

Let death seize upon them, and let them go down quick into hell: for wickedness is in their dwellings, and among them.

As for me, I will call upon God; and the LORD shall save me.

Evening, and morning, and at noon, will I pray, and cry aloud: and he shall hear my voice.

He hath delivered my soul in peace from the battle that was against me: for there were many with me.

God shall hear, and afflict them, even he that abideth of old. Because they have no changes, therefore they fear not God.

He hath put forth his hands against such as be at peace with him: he hath broken his covenant.

The words of his mouth were smoother than butter, but war was in his heart: his words were softer than oil, yet were they drawn swords.

Cast thy burden upon the LORD, and he shall sustain thee: he shall never suffer the righteous to be moved.

But thou, O God, shalt bring them down into the pit of destruction: bloody and deceitful men shall not live out half their days; but I will trust in thee. *(Ps. 55:1–23).*

There is someone reading this today, God had you get to this chapter because He loves you and He wants the best for your life. He is saying right now: "STOP reading for a few minutes and begin to pray: *"Father, I am a sinner and I need you in my Life. I believe that Jesus Christ is your son and He died, was buried and rose from the dead to save me from my sins. I'm sorry for the things I have done in my flesh that caused hurt and pain in other's lives and I repent of my sins. Lord I give you charge of my life. Thank you Lord for saving me."* In Jesus name.

Each of us now must put on our night-vision glasses so that we can see the enemy coming. He is coming, and he stands at the door seeking entry into your mind garden, the mind garden of your family, and the mind garden of your friends and enemies. He just might be standing next to you right now. This is why we must be discerners of the hearts of those with whom we come into contact with daily. Satan does not want you to read and study the word of God. He wants you to be like Solomon during mating season. Satan wants you to get caught up in the flow in a media stream, a self-stream, and a world stream. As you repent of your sins and turn your life around and start putting Christ first in your life, Satan uses these streams to hinder your movement towards God. Remember in chapter 9 I told you that God draws you to Christ? When you find yourself in the rapids of life flowing down hill, remember, you don't have to stress. Just relax in the word of God and He will draw you up stream into His presence.

Satan wants you to feed on death and destruction in this fight. He wants to wear you down as you push against the backward stream of darkness and move upstream to the light of God. But your daily reading and studying of God's word equips you with the necessary armor to withstand the attacks of Satan on your mind. Your leap for joy will propel you into the arms of your Savior and Lord, and not into the arms of the devourer. I pray that you are getting this. As you leap into His arms, you will no longer need the night vision glasses for you will have leaped into the light of His love for you.

Let us no longer complain about our sufferings. Let us rejoice in the opportunity to be a witness on the battlefield for our God. Keep our souls unspotted, unwrinkled, unblemished from the tricks of Satan. We are more than conquerors through Christ Jesus. Let the world hear your war cry. Let the heavens hear your war cry, and let Satan hear your war cry. Today you put Satan on notice, for he has no power to fight a warrior of God. As we end this chapter, lets us pray:

> *"Be merciful unto me, O God, for man would swallow me up. He is fighting daily against me. He is attempting to oppress me. If they could, my enemies would daily swallow me up, for they are many that fight against me. In you, O lord, I will praise. I will praise your word. In you I have put my trust. I will not be afraid of what man can do unto me. Your word is upon me and in me. I will render praise unto you. You have delivered my soul from death. You will also deliver my feet from falling so that I can walk before you in the light of the living. Lord, I thank you for preparing my armor for battle. I am well fitted to fight the enemy of my soul. Amen!"*

CHAPTER 16
Spiritual Warfare–Your Destiny

As we work to win the spiritual warfare that attempts to saturate our mind with negative thoughts, negative feelings, and negative emotions, we must be willing to give our lives over to God and trust Him to lead us. God wants to heal all our past scars, all our past setbacks, and all of the letdowns and disappointments that have catapulted us into depressed states. All of us have heard of Him, have talked about Him, and yes, have ignored His call on our lives. And because of that choice, we have found ourselves in a battle against our own selves.

Proverbs 16:2 tells us: "All the ways of a man are clean in his own eyes, but the Lord weigheth the spirits." *Verse 3* reads: "Commit thy works unto the Lord and thy thoughts shall be established."

How we see things will either drive us to or drive us away from our destiny. Note that this second verse says that God weighs the spirits. The word *spirits* is plural in this passage. It denotes more than one. When it refers to Satan, it is like being jumped on by a gang of thugs and murderous demons. You come out of the fight all bloody and dazed, and if you develop any fear or have doubt in your heart, you could lose your life, your eternal life. You know the scripture passage: "The thief cometh not but to steal, and to kill, and to destroy:" (*John 10b*). If you are saved today and have God's light shining in your life, Satan has centered his whole arsenal on you. Please believe me; you are his next target. We, the church, the body of Christ are under spiritual terrorist attack.

When was the last time you had a thought in your mind that had no God in it? Trust me, it was just before this chapter. You negatively saw, you heard, you felt, or you thought very briefly about something or someone that planted a subliminal seed deep in the garden of your mind, waiting for the next attack of Satan to water it and his next attack to give it life. If it didn't happen just before you started this chapter, Satan has shifted the purpose of my statement on the subject to cause some of you to go there in thought jut now. This is how he operates. Rebuke it now in the name of Jesus.

God tells us in *Proverbs 19:20* to: "Hear counsel and receive instruction that thou may be wise in thy latter end." Too often we allow time to help us to forget the impact of that last trial, the pains of past tribulations, and we faithfully walk back into the enemy's camp unarmed.

We don't heed the instructions of *Ephesians 6:11:* "Put on the whole armor of God that ye may be able to stand against the wiles of the devil." God told us to trust in Him; *Proverbs 3:5* states: "Trust in the Lord with all thine heart and lean not unto thine own understanding." But we are so quick to put our trust in man and not in God. The word of God enables us to discern the true intentions of people. It gives us an inward track on the spiritual motives, if any, of the individual in front of us. If we walked more in the spirit and not in our flesh, we would not satisfy the lust of the flesh, and we would stand ready to minister to everyone God puts in front of us. We will know who not to and who to witness to. God will always present them to us at the appointed time. God is preparing the soul in the minds of men to hear from you. We must be ready to hear from God.

Answer this question: What do you understand about life? Trust me, you know nothing. If you can say that you know God with the evidence of a changed nature toward God, then you are on a stronger foundation than most. But so many are clueless about life. Why do I say this? It is because unless you are in God and God is in you, you have no life, for God is life. Your existence is that of a heathen worshiping and fearing everything in the natural. You know God is life, don't you? Then let me say it like this:

Unless you are in life and life is in you, you cannot know, have, or possess life. You cannot know, have or possess God.

Life is to know God and to have God in control of your being. You have to give your life to Him in order to have life, for the life that you live now outside of Him is not life—it is death. In order to have life, something in you has to die. Your heart and your thinking must line up with every word that comes out of the mouth of God, for His word is life. This is why we should seek God while it is day, while we are young. When we get to the point that we think we are grown, when we think we are so mature that we are in the position to make constructive decisions on our own about our existence, we swing open wide the door of self, and Satan walks in, takes a seat, and becomes your best friend. That's called sleeping with the enemy. But when we put God first, we understand that we don't have the answers—He does—and we yield our lives in total submission to His perfect will for us. We die to ourselves, and we live for Him. I am not saying that when you come into the knowledge of God's existence when you are older, you have many ungodly habits and thoughts that have to die. I am saying, though, that your withdrawal from the world's system can be a little harder if you are not truly committed to God. Let's be honest. There are somethings in this world that are not good for you but you have accepted them as necessary evils in your life.

Everyone has a destiny. Everyone has a purpose. Knowing what they are and doing them are two different things. Take a two-year-old child as an example. You tell this child not to go near or touch the hot stove. You tell him over and over and over again. When the stove is warm, you even put his hands on it and remove them, hoping the message sinks in but it doesn't. His hand wasn't on the hot stove long enough to feel its true heat. If you had left his hand on the stove long enough, it would have been called child abuse.

So you think you got your point across, and in time, the child burns himself on the hot stove deliberately. Your telling him of the danger wasn't enough. He had to experience the heat, burn his skin, and feel unnecessary pain in order to fully understand the consequences of his actions for not following your instruction. Sounds like Eve, doesn't it? Sounds like Adam too, correct? It also sounds like each of us.

There are some who don't believe in Satan and in how he works. They don't believe because he, like God, doesn't operate in the physical realm like we do; since those who don't believe can't see him, they choose to believe he doesn't exist. Thank God for *Romans 8:28*, which reads: "And we know that all things work together for good to them that love God, to them who are the called according to His purpose." God has a purpose for each of us. We have a job to do for His kingdom. Satan knows that when we walk in our purpose, when we live out our destiny in accordance to our life in Christ, Satan is defeated, and we are the victors.

Romans 8:29 reads: "For whom He did foreknow, He also did predestinate to be conformed to the image of His son, that He might be the firstborn among many brethren." The word of God tells us that God knew us before He formed us in our mother's womb; and before we came forth out of the womb, He sanctified us and ordained us (*Jer. 1:5*). This scripture is specifically talking about Jeremiah, but it also applies to each of us. God has predestined our destiny, and He has sanctified and ordained us to go to the nations with this good news—the Gospel.

If you don't mind, I'd like for you to read a few scriptures.

> Blessed is the man who walks not in the counsel of the ungodly, nor stands in the way of sinners, nor sits in the seat of the scornful.
>
> But his delight is in the law of the Lord; and in his law doeth he mediate day and night
>
> And he shall be like a tree planted by the rivers of water, that brings forth its fruit in its season; its leaf also shall not wither; and whatsoever he doth shall prosper.
>
> The ungodly are not so, but are like the chaff which the wind drive away.
>
> Therefore, the ungodly shall not stand in the judgment, nor sinners in the congregation of the righteous.

For the Lord knows the ways of the righteous; but the way of the ungodly shall perish (*Ps. 1:1–6*).

When we take counsel with God, our destiny becomes fixed. Nothing on this earth or below this earth can change that. We delight in all things that are good and build a strong foundation for our lives in the soil of God's Word. God knows our ways because each and every day of our lives, He draws us to Him. He talks to us in the stillness of our surroundings, and we listen. We listen because we know that He is the source of our eternal nourishment. He and only He can give us life.

Blessed is the man who trusteth in the Lord, and whose hope the Lord is.

For he shall be like a tree planted by the waters and that spreads out her roots by the river, and shall not see when heat come, but her leaf shall be green; and shall not be anxious in the year of drought, neither shall cease from yielding fruit.

The heart is deceitful above all things and desperately wicked; who can know it?

I, the Lord, search the heart, I test the conscience, even to give every man according to his way, and according to the fruit of his doings (*Jer. 17:7–10*).

When Satan sees that you have made a commitment to follow God, he will send you trials and tribulations in an attempt to discredit your faith. God's desire for you to fulfill your destiny is so dear to Him that when He sees that you are moving in the wrong direction, He will send you a test—something that will show you that you are about to travel down the wrong path. You, however, have to put your trust in Him, discern, and know the difference. The question then is, "How can I put my faith in God, whom I can't see, or in man, who means me no good?" God says in *verse 5* of this same scripture: "Thus says the Lord, Cursed be the man that trust in man, and makes flesh his arm, and whose heart depart from the Lord."

He curses anyone or anything that would attempt to draw you away from Him. *Matthew 23:27* reads: "Woe unto you scribes and Pharisees, hypocrites! For you are like whited sepulchers [graves], which indeed appear beautiful outwardly, but are within full of dead men's bones, and of all uncleanness."

God wants you to hold your head up and walk into your destiny. He loves you, and He wants the best for your life. Even while this world is attempting to persuade you that its way is better, you feel the drawing of God for a change in your life. He is saying right now, "Come to Me. I will give you rest and lead you into your promised destiny."

Your next decision will be the one that determines your destiny with Satan or your destiny with God. What's so real about it is that no one can make the decision but you. The only person that you have right now to aid you in making the right decision is the Holy Spirit. Which destiny will you choose? If you don't mind, take a few minutes here and pray for yourself. I and all the sons and daughters of God are rooting for you and for the prosperity of your soul.

THE HOLY SPIRIT CONNECTION

Have you heard it said, "No man is an island"? There are two types of islands on this planet, *continental islands* and *oceanic islands*. Continental islands are bodies of land that lie on the continental shelf of a continent. Oceanic islands are ones that do not sit on continental shelves. The vast majority of oceanic islands are volcanic in origin. With these definitions of an island, how could a man be an island? He is sitting/resting on something. From these definitions, a man island must be connected to something. So our statement becomes a metaphor that makes it applicable to its application. Each of us are islands connected to something. In metaphor, we rest on a continental shelf (Christ), or we were spawned from a volcano (Satan). Either way, we are connected.

However, when the storms of life hit, our ability to withstand the turbulence will be determined by what and whom we are connected to.

The Garden of Your Mind

In birth, each of us was connected to the life-giving bloodstream of our mothers through the placenta. God designed the process of nurturing the unborn from the mother through the uterine and from the uterine to the placenta. Everything that we needed to sustain us was supplied to us through the placenta. Through this placenta, we were connected in layers to our mother. This was an internal connection.

At birth externally, we are connected to our mother due to our inability to operate effectively in our new environment. We have no cognitive abilities to function on our own. If we were to spend too much time away from our external support at this stage in our lives, we would die. We are totally dependent on our parent(s) to nurture us into maturity—a maturity that hopefully causes us to be cognitively capable of making right decisions for our future. As in the natural, so it is in the spiritual.

Each of us should be connected to Christ through the Holy Spirit. It is the Holy Spirit that guides us into all truth and righteous thinking. He keeps us from the wicked one, keeps us at peace in the midst of storms, and teaches us the ways of sonship in God. Many churches have replaced the Holy Spirit with technology. They feel that they don't have to spend time in prayer and fasting. Everything we need to study the Bible, teach a Bible class, and preach can be obtained on the Internet. Someone has already done the research. But their research applied to their ability to discern the move of God. We need a word for today. Life situations today are not like they were ten, fifteen, twenty, twenty-five, fifty years ago. As the environment of this world is changing, the wisdom of the Holy Spirit is waiting for us to make the right request so that He can open our minds to deeper revelations on the move of God.

Just like with Solomon, God wants to give you something. You have to choose wisely and, like King David, walk in truth, in righteousness, and in uprightness of heart. When you seek after the heart of God, He will seek after you. He wants to give you the desires of your heart. Jesus sent the Comforter (Holy Spirit) into the world to abide with us and in us. His sole purpose is to lead us into all truth. We connect to the godhead when we connect to the Holy Spirit. He gives us wisdom to pull down the satanic strongholds in our lives. He gives us boldness to witness the love of God for mankind. He gives us strength to stand against the temptations from Satan and the lust in our flesh. He also gives us knowledge to go through the test that God sends our way to prepare us for His next move in our life. Boy, talk about favor.

Then came there two women, who were harlots, unto the king, and stood before him.

And the one woman said, O my lord, I and this woman dwell in one house, and I was delivered of a child with her in the house.

And it come to pass the third day after that I was delivered, that this woman was delivered also, and we were together. There was no stranger with us in the house [except] we two were in the house.

And this woman's child died in the night, because she [lay on] it.

And she arose at midnight and took my son from beside me, while thine handmaid slept, and laid it in her bosom, and laid her dead child in my bosom.

And when I rose in the morning to [nurse my child], behold it was dead; but when I had [looked at] it in the morning, behold, it was not my son whom I did bear.

And the other woman said, Nay; but the living child is my son, and the dead is thy son. And this said, No; but the dead child is thy son, and the living is my son. Thus they spoke before the king.

Then said the king, The one saith, This is my son who liveth, and thy son is the dead; and the other saith, Nay: but thy son is the dead child, and my son is the living.

And the king said, Bring me a sword. And thay brought a sword before the king.

And the king said, Divide the living child in two, and give half to the one, and half to the other.

Then spoke the woman whose the living child was unto the king, for her [hart yearned over] her son, and she said, O my lord, give her the living child, and [by no means] slay it. But the other said, Let it be neither mine nor thine, but divide it.

Then the king answered and said, Give her the living child, and [by no means] slay it; she is the mother of it.

And all Israel heard of the judgment which the king had judged, and they feared the king; for they say that the wisdom of God was in him, to do [justice]. *1 Kings 3:16-18.*

How many of you will agree with me that wisdom and the proper use of it can heal the wounds inflected on God's people? Many of you may be familiar with this story and its outcome. In *1 Kings 3:9*, Solomon asked God to "Give, therefore, thy servant an understanding heart to judge thy people, that I may discern between good and evil. For who is able to judge this they great people?" Solomon's pursuit for wisdom and not wealth pleased God. At so young an age, he know that his rulership over God's people demanded wisdom, not wealth.

"Discern between good and evil." This statement is the key that unlocks the door to our spiritual destiny. Solomon didn't want to be like God. He wanted to be able to judge God's people in accordance to the wisdom that God gave him. What makes his request different from Eve's desire is that he requested this wisdom from God. Eve attempted to take it from God. *Wisdom cannot be taken; it can only be given.* When we move into an intimate relationship with Christ, we move into an intimate relationship with God. When we move into an intimate relationship with God, we move into an intimate relationship with the Holy Spirit. When we move into an intimate relationship with the Holy Spirit, we move into an intimate relationship with one another. Like Solomon, when we move from the darkness of our own wisdom and move into the light of the wisdom of God, His Spirit gives us treasures of knowledge to defeat all of the tricks of the enemy.

Your free will places you in the driver's seat. You need to get out of the driver's seat and *will* your destiny to God. In the natural we will things to people to have after we die. You must will your life to God, in the spirit, while you are in the earth realm, so that He can give you eternal life. Give Him full authority to take over the affairs of your transition from death to eternal life with Him. Whatever you need from Him, He is ready to supply it. When you give your life to Him, He gives eternity to you. All you have to do is put down your will and pick up His will for your life—right now; you don't have to wait any longer. As Solomon asked and God gave him more than what he asked for, you too have to ask God for what you want. Choose wisely. Remember, it's your destiny in Jesus' name.

It is not by happenstance that you picked this book to read. It is not by happenstance that you read it. The favor of God is upon your life. He has predestined you to be here right now receiving the wisdom needed to move into your destiny. What is the next move for your life? I can't answer that for you. You might not be able to answer it either right now. But God can and He knows the plans He has for you. As you close this book and view the back cover, close your eyes and ask God for guidance. Talk to Him and listen to what He has to say. He has been wanting to talk to you and share with you all of the exciting things He has planned for you.

You are His child and He wants to satisfy your need for righteous living. He wants to show you how to overcome you so that you can overcome the world and take dominion over it. The world that has been discussed here is the world inside your mind. Every waking moment of your life from this day forward, you must allow the Holy Spirit to till the soil of your mind so that He may plant good seed deep into the soul of your mind. Every day that you postpone having your mind gardened by God is another day Satan works to build strongholds in your garden.

If you are to be like Christ, you need to become the fruit in the garden. Check your spirit daily to confirm if you are becoming the fruit in the spirit: love, joy, peace, long-suffering, gentleness, goodness, faith, meekness, and self-control. As the fruit in the garden, allow the husbandman to plant your seeds into the garden of others. As you produce for God you will build a kingdom like no other. A kingdom without weeds.

NOTES

Introduction

1. Richard Yeakley, National Council of Churches *Yearbook of American and Canadian Churches USA New Letter* February 14, 2011, P. 12.

2. Bill Smalt, "Why People Leave the Church," *Ministry Today Magazine*", http://ministrytodaymag.com/leadership/ethics/1068-why-people-leave-the-church. April 30, 2001.

Chapter 2
Here's Mud in Your Other I—Fear

1. "Don't Run from Jezebel," David Wilkerson, World Challenge Pulpit Series, http://www.tscpulpitseries.org/english/1990s/ts930802.html, Last Modified August 2, 1993.

2. "Who Invented the Wheel and Axle," Mark Zorn, VISIONLAUNCH.com, June 14, 2014.

3. Mark Bastiaan van Iersel, "A Reader-Response Commentary," *Continuum International* (1998), p. 167.

Chapter 3
Kingdom Preschool

1. "Preschool Fears: Why they happen and what to do." Melanie Haken's interview with Patricia Henderson Shimm, Babycenter.com. 1997-2015.

Chapter 4
The Facts of Life

1. "What's the Difference Between Broilers, Fryers, Roasters and Other Sizes of Chickens?" Emma Christensen, www.thekitchen.com, April 21, 2014

2. "Lust," Wikipedia, https://en.wikipedia.org/wiki/lust, Last Modified September 16,

3. "Addiction," https://en.wikipedia.org/wiki/Addiction, Wikipedia, Last Modified October 21, 2015.

Chapter 8
Your Wilderness Test

1. "Wilderness," Merriam-Webster, Last Modified 2015, http://www.merriam-webster.com/dictionary/wilderness.

Chapter 10
A Need to Read

1. "Read," Merriam-Webster, Last Modified 2015, http://www.merriaam-webster.com/dictionary/read.

Chapter 15
Spiritual Warfare—Your Armor

1. Dr. Edward F. Murphy, *The Handbook for Spiritual Warfare* (Nashville: Thomas Nelson, 1996), p. 98.

www.ingramcontent.com/pod-product-compliance
Lightning Source LLC
Chambersburg PA
CBHW022105160426
43198CB00008B/356